THE CHARACTER OF THE CUSTOMER

a story from the *Method Marketing Files* of Stan Islavski

The perfect *method* for connecting with customers

Bruce Labovitz

Brian Regli, Ph.D.

iUniverse, Inc.
Bloomington

The Character of the Customer
A story from the Method Marketing files of Stan Islavski

iUniverse books may be ordered through booksellers or by contacting:

iUniverse
1663 Liberty Drive
Bloomington, IN 47403
www.iuniverse.com
1-800-Authors (1-800-288-4677)

ISBN: 978-1-4502-3659-1 (pbk)
ISBN: 978-1-4502-3661-4 (cloth)
ISBN: 978-1-4502-3660-7 (ebk)

Printed in the United States of America

iUniverse rev. date: 11/19/10

Table of Contents

Introduction

The book you are about to read is based on the simple belief that marketing is about more than an academic understanding of the principles of business. The premise of the authors is that it is possible to teach marketers to connect a company and its products with markets and customers using a technique that outlines the ways actors make emotional connections with the characters they are preparing to portray. The book is intended to impart to its readers a means for connecting with the character of customers. It's about finding new ways of relating to customer and marketplace needs and motivations. The technique outlined throughout this story is intended to teach the reader how to anticipate the reaction of customers when presented with the ever changing circumstances of a competitive marketplace. This book is about applying an inter-disciplinary approach to a long-standing and proven technique in an attempt to innovate and advance the marketing process.

The authors of this story have been friends for over thirty-five years, having grown up together outside Philadelphia. As kids we had sports in common and as we grew older we both developed an interest in the arts. As young men we performed in numerous theatrical productions, both dramatic and musical, in a variety of venues. We both studied acting in one way or another through formal classes and anecdotal learning. Ironically, however, we have never performed in a production together.

Both of us left for college to conquer the world. Bruce studied business at New York University's Leonard Stern School of Business, earning dual degrees in Economics and Marketing. Brian studied international relations and performed at Georgetown before earning a Ph.D. at age twenty-five from the Fletcher School of International Relations at Tufts. We both lived abroad early on with Bruce studying at Tel Aviv University and Brian teaching at the University of Prague and subsequently living and studying in modern day Russia.

After school we both embarked on careers in business, Bruce as a pre-Internet computer information management systems entrepreneur starting his first of several businesses and Brian as an international business consultant. After exiting his second business, Bruce joined Brian, who was returning to the US after two years of working in Mexico City at Telmex, to found an innovative start-up telecommunications business developing a revolutionary convergent primary line and data traffic voice-over-IP network in high-density residential communities.

After the dot-com and telecommunications meltdown we embarked down different paths with Bruce executing an IPO as Chief Financial Officer for a real estate company and Brian founding Drakontas, a government services contractor focusing on law enforcement technology. Brian is currently the company's CEO. Bruce is now Managing Director and Chief Financial Officer of ADR Software in Reston, Virginia.

We wrote the first draft of this novel in 1997 as an adventure, an exploration of our creative sides. At the time, our motivation for writing the book was simply that it seemed like a fun idea to document our method marketing theory in a lighthearted and satirical manner. After writing the story we submitted it to several traditional publishing houses but were not successful in our efforts to get the manuscript sold. Over the past ten years, as we've grown both professional and personally, we have periodically revisited the manuscript and each time we found that the story and its teaching continued to be compelling, relevant and above all, entertaining. So after ten years, we decided to "freshen it up" and self-publish the book to share our story and idea with the world.

When it comes to acting skills we are fortunate to have had the opportunity over the years to learn informally from other more experienced voices with regard to acting tools and techniques. This book centers on the work of Constantin Stanislavski, the father of Method Acting. Stanislavski was born in Moscow, Russia, in 1863. After acting in a variety of roles and productions in his youth, Stanislavski founded the Moscow Art Theater in his late thirty's. His reasons for founding the company as stated in his autobiography *My Life in Art* are as follows:

> *"In order to rejuvenate the art, we declared war on all the conventionalities of the theater wherever they might occur—in the acting, in the properties, in the scenery, the costumes, the interpretation of the play, the curtain, or anywhere else in the theater. All that was new and that violated the usual customs of the theater seemed beautiful and useful to us."*

Stanislavski lived in a period of great social change, and was attempting to make theater more "real" in its approach to the events portrayed on the stage. Instead of gaudy costumes and artificial vocal cadences, he emphasized what is now referred to more commonly as "getting into character." Through his involvement with the Art Theater and other subsequent ventures, he developed what today is considered the definitive statement of technique for the modern actor commonly referred to simply as "the method," although Stanislavski was more comfortable calling it "the system."

The revolutionary period that gave birth to his art also forced Stanislavski's departure from Russia after the Communist takeover. Russia's loss was our gain, though. His exile in the United States and Europe gave him the incentive to formalize his system in writing. He took the opportunity to educate a contingent of young American actors who, in turn, expanded his thinking and techniques further. More than one hundred years after his birth, actors and playwrights still begin any discussion of acting techniques with a reference to Stanislavski, even if it is to later disagree and suggest revisions to Stanislavski's thought.

Stanislavski is certainly not the only source for information about acting techniques, but this is not a book about acting. Our goal is to give you a straightforward approach to how acting can make a difference in building marketing and communications strategy. So we've decided to bring Stanislavski back to life and have him personally guide you through his technique in story form. You'll have to give us a bit of literary license in the process. Because theater and performance art are, according to many, based on a "willing suspension of disbelief," our hope is that you will be able to suspend disbelief and allow yourself to believe in our characters and their teachings.

At the same time, this book is more than a story. Each chapter provides a concrete definition of an acting concept and a straightforward discussion of how the concept can form the basis for communications programming and activities in a corporate environment. By the end of the book, our hope is that you will have a series of tools which you can use, either formally or informally, both discretely and in the aggregate, to think about customers and purchasing behaviors. As you read, you may find it helpful to read the postscript of each chapter both before and after you read the narrative of the chapter. If that's the case, don't worry its not cheating.

We have drawn on a number of sources to illustrate our ideas. Portions of this account are taken from the writings and autobiography of Constantin Stanislavski, including *My Life in Art* (Little, Brown & Company, 1924) and *An Actor Prepares, Building a Character and Creating a Role* (Routledge/Theater Art Books, 1988). Additional information comes from *Acting: A Handbook of the Stanislavski Method*, compiled by Tony Cole (Crown Publishers, 1985) and *A Practical Handbook for the Actor* (Vintage Books, 1974).

Many thanks go to our supportive wives, Katie and Tanya, who have not only indulged us in this decade long project but have provided us with support, motivation and love throughout the past twenty years. We would be remiss if we didn't also thank our children Jenny, Jacob and Sarah (Bruce) and Gabriel and Andrea (Brian), four of whom were not born when we started this project but all of whom have offered inspiration in one form or another along the way.

This book is dedicated in loving memory of Dr. Deborah Labovitz, a role model and inspiration to both of us.

Preface

All the world's a stage

Other than the theater, there is nowhere that we know of where that is truer than in business. Business is about successfully connecting your company, its products and its services with the demand profiles and consumption motivations of consumers in your marketplace. Acting is about identifying the motivations of a character and understanding how that character will respond to circumstances within the context of a particular moment, a specific scene and the continuum of an entire story.

This book presents a new way to think about the relationship between marketing professionals, their companies, the clients they work for and the customers they serve. A straightforward business school class on marketing can teach the tangible principles (the 4 Ps, market research, statistical analysis, etc.), but the real challenge is teaching the most intangible principle of all. The quintessential question to answer is: ***how can you, your organization and your products better connect with the character of your customer?***

Some people say that when it comes to business and connecting with customers either you have a gut instinct for it or you don't. You will often hear it said that you're either a natural at marketing and sales or you're not. But is that true? Is it that absolute or is there actually a way to teach the intangible skills? There's the academic approach, but that ignores the emotional connection of marketing. This book asks (and hopefully answers) the basic question of: ***how do you teach a marketer to truly connect with the character of their customer?***

Before Stanislavski came along, the same thing was often said about acting. Prior to the Stanislavski Method, people wondered if acting was merely something you were born with or whether it could be taught. Stanislavski argued that natural ability can only take you so far, and that excellence in acting required a constant focus on a rigorous technique. In fact, to Stanislavski, people with limited "natural talent" often make the best actors because they have to work harder to achieve more.

In this "script" the same argument is made about marketing. The story proffers the notion that excellence in marketing can be supported by a technique that teaches the intangible, "softer" side of the marketing discipline. If marketing professionals are looking for ways to identify the "character of the customer," what better place to start than with a technique that focuses entirely on character, motivation, and individual action?

This book has been written for a broad audience of professionals with a general interest in both business and marketplace activities. At the same time, we believe that the premise and practice of method marketing offers a potential competitive advantage for corporate managers whose daily activity involves sales, advertising, marketing, product development or any other communications discipline. By helping other people in your organization apply basic acting techniques to their everyday marketplace decisions, the technique of method marketing will promote improved understanding of your customers' needs and interests and will help facilitate exchanges and transactions.

The story you are about to read is meant to be about an idea and a technique and it can be applied to any business environment. As such, the business of the company which serves as the backdrop for this story is intentionally left vague and ambiguous. It is not our intention to limit the breadth and scope of the applicability of the method marketing concept by framing it in any one specific vertical market.

With that said, we invite you to suspend disbelief while we raise the curtain on our opening night production of *The Character of the Customer*. Please sit back, relax, switch your cell phones to silent mode and remember, no flash photography is permitted during the performance.

Enjoy the show!

Prologue

"Now it all makes sense," she said dramatically as she gave him a big hug and a gentle kiss on the check.

The sentence she had uttered just moments before echoed in her mind as she stood there, alone in the hallway, trying to collect herself after hearing the news of his true identity. Looking back over the past several months it all seemed so obvious. How could she have missed it? There were all of the analogies and anecdotes. There were the references to plays, actors, characters and directors. And most of all, he didn't seem to know a thing about the academic aspects of marketing. But now, alone with her thoughts in the hallway outside the executive suite, she stood to receive the biggest promotion of her career and ascend to the job she had been trying to earn for some time now. She realized, as she reflected on her time with *Stan*, that it was all because of his unorthodox approach, and his tireless commitment to his *technique*.

Out of sheer exhaustion she sat down on one of the comfortable chairs nearby to wait it out. It was out of her hands now. The presentation to the committee had gone well. She smiled silently as she recalled his insistence about referring to it as a production. At this point, all she could do was wait to see if she had *landed the part*.

Scene I

The Actor's Challenge

Our story begins with a meeting between a theater person and a business person as two people come to realize that their approaches to their respective professions are very similar.

* * * *

"Stop! You can't just go in there without an appointment!"

The secretary spoke with a tone of authority that would have stopped most people dead in their tracks. Since this man did not know the protocols of the corporate world, however, the protest had no diminishing effect on his determination. He passed by her desk, opened the door and walked directly into the office of the CEO.

"I'm here to accept position of Director," he announced with a confident sounding Slavic accent as he entered the room. "I am responding to advertisement in newspaper for position of Director of Theater Company."

The CEO looked up, somewhat startled by the accent and broken English, to see a man in what appeared to be a costume of some sort; glasses almost like antiques with graying hair and distinctive Slavic features that supported the accent. The secretary was right on the man's heels, and was about to insist that the man depart immediately when the CEO stopped her with a look of curiosity that she had seen many times before. The CEO composed himself and asked the obvious question.

"You're here for a position? What position?"

"The position of Director, of course," the man responded, reaching out to shake the CEO's hand before taking a seat opposite the standing CEO. With an air of confidence he said "I am Constantin Stanislavski. Of course, you are familiar with my work."

The CEO made a quick mental scan through his contacts trying to recall all of the people he had worked with in the past. His blank stare betrayed his usual confidence. "How exactly would I have heard of you? Have we worked together before?"

"I don't believe so," the man responded. "The majority of my work was in Russia, in Moscow." He paused a moment to determine if the man in front of him was showing any signs of recognition. He was not. "After revolution, I came..."

"Revolution?" interrupted the CEO.

"The Communists, of course." responded the man. "After revolution I was no longer able to work in Russia. I could not perform my work so I flee to United States where I begin to record my method."

"Your method? Your method on what?" he inquired rather puzzled.

"Acting! My methods on acting and directing."

The conversation stopped dead. The secretary broke the silence by asking, in a somewhat anxious tone, "Should I be calling security, sir?"

As she asked the question, an expression of amazement and disbelief passed across the CEO's face. "Wait a minute," he said softly not quite believing he was about to say what he was about to say. "Stanislavski. Do you mean *the* Stanislavski? The father of Method Acting?" He really couldn't believe what he had just said.

"Yes," the man said somewhat annoyed that it had taken so long but at the same time he beamed with the pride of a person who had been recognized. "You *have* heard of me." His command of the English language seemed to be improving as the conversation continued.

"Well who hasn't?" The CEO gestured politely for the secretary to leave the room, adding "It's ok, I do know this man, sort of. You can shut the door behind you. Thanks." As the confused secretary departed, the CEO continued his praise. "Anyone involved in the theater knows of the great Stanislavski and the theory of Method Acting. I took a theater studies course in college and I acted in a few community theater productions back when I had more free time. I guess you could characterize me as," now it was the CEO's turn to stumble briefly searching for the word he was looking for, "as a ... a fan."

9

"Then this is settled." Stanislavski quipped back. "What production will we will start with?"

"Production?" The CEO's confused expression returned in earnest. "What are you talking about?" he replied.

"Do you not remember your own advertisement? Here, I have a copy of it with me. It reads: *Directors position available at Theater Company*. Stanislavski pulled out a copy of the newspaper and handed it to the CEO. The CEO's eyes focused immediately on the listing circled in red. "If you have had any experience in the theater, as you claim you have, you know that my Method Acting technique provides the best tools available for a production company. I come to offer my services."

After seeing the typo in the ad he had just been shown, the CEO knew what was going on. He gestured half-heartedly in an attempt to stop Stanislavski, but the effort was to no avail.

"The method is very simple, really." The Slavic accent remained but the English seemed to have inexplicably improved to near perfection. It reminded the CEO of the moment in the movie *The Hunt for Red October* when the dialog changes from all Russian to perfect English. Given what seemed to be going on around him, he figured that this transformation was the least of his worries.

Without missing a beat Stanislavski continued, "Its purpose is to serve as a framework for teaching actors how to know their characters and connect themselves with the material presented. It has three parts. First, each member of the company, as well as the company as a whole, must understand what is inside themselves, their emotions, their range and their acting capabilities. That's the *inner*. Once the inner is understood, the actor gets to know his character. That's the second discipline, the *external*. The motivations and the history are all part of developing a specific character which is in alignment with the inner capabilities of the actor. The third discipline is that of *synthesis*. Each actor, and the company as a whole, brings together the inner learning and the external knowledge of the characters to create a complete production process. And throughout the process there's *rehearsal*, a time to share ideas and work together to improve our individual and collective performances. Surely these ideas are of interest to you and to your production company."

The CEO broke in. "Mr. Stanislavski..."

"Call me Constantin."

"Alright, Constantin, I think there has been some confusion. You said *theater company*, right? It appears that there has been a typographic error in the listing. We are The Atre Company and we are looking for a Director. But the position is for Director of Marketing. It appears that they left out the space and cut off the words *of Marketing* in the title."

Confused and suddenly feeling somewhat discouraged, Stanislavski simply replied, "Oh, I am most sorry." His disappointment seemed genuine to the CEO.

But the CEO was far from discouraged. He was hearing words and ideas which he recognized even though they were coming from this man who obviously had no clue he was connecting with a potential employer.

Stanislavski had risen and begun to collect his things when the CEO stopped him. "Wait a minute, repeat the three parts of the method again."

Now more confused, Stanislavski seated himself back into the chair and started over. "The first challenge is an internal one, where the actor must become intimately familiar with himself and his inventory of resources..."

"Sounds like personal skills, core competencies and corporate resources," the CEO interrupted.

Stanislavski paused, giving the CEO a slightly peculiar look and continued. "The second element is external, where the actor studies the character and develops an understanding of the motivations of the character..."

"That's getting to know your customers and markets," the CEO again interrupted.

"...and the third element is a synthesis..."

Not waiting for the explanation the CEO interrupted again saying, "Which is applying your discipline to producing appropriate products and services to present to your target markets with appropriately supportive communications. Perfect! The analogy works!"

Now Stanislavski was really confused. "Now what are *you* talking about?" he asked in a somewhat sheepish tone.

"Here's my situation," the CEO began. "This company's in trouble. That's why I'm here. Somewhere along the way we've lost our way. We no longer connect with our customers and markets. I was hired about six months ago to turn this company around, refocus it on core markets, solidify our market position, increase transactional revenues and restore shareholder value. I don't know how much you know about running a production like this, but there's a great deal that goes into restructuring, refocusing and reorienting a business. Over the past six months I've done everything the textbook tells you to do. I've set targets for return on investment. I've challenged everyone to increase sales. I've arranged to sell off some of our underperforming assets. I've travelled to all of our facilities to meet with our people. I've tried to align our offerings with the demand of the marketplace and above all I've tried to identify a niche in which to succeed. I think that last one has been the most challenging for me. We're working through the strategy process right now for cutting costs among our profitable lines. We're going to hire some people and unfortunately fire others. It's going to be difficult, but I believe that with the right leadership and innovative practices we will emerge a leaner, stronger and more focused organization."

Now it was Stanislavski's turn to exhibit a bewildered look that betrayed his confidence.

"Here's the problem," the CEO grimaced. "We don't have the marketing support we need and as a group we don't have the right," he paused as he again searched for the right words. "Collective character, I guess that's a good way to describe it." He searched Stanislavski's face for reassurance that did not materialize. The CEO continued, apparently undeterred by the bizarre situation that was unfolding around him. "The marketing director I inherited here had no vision for what this company was, where it could go or how to connect with our customers. I fired him. I've interviewed three prospective candidates since then but I didn't feel like any of them could connect with us as an organization. Truth is, they were all the same. They talk about the markets but they don't understand them. They confuse marketing with advertising and advertising with selling. I haven't heard any breakthrough thinking. I've even searched internally for a candidate. There's one person I really like, but before

13

she will be ready for the job she's got to break out of the textbook world in which she operates and learn more about how to *contribute* to this process I've initiated. I'd like to have the opportunity to promote her in a few months once we're back on track, but I don't have time to train her myself."

After a deep breath and a chance to plan his next move he continued.

"Basically, I need an angle. I need to find someone who'll think outside the proverbial box we all live in here. I need some solid, strategic direction for our marketing and communications teams and frankly I need it right now."

The CEO laughed and changed his tone. "So, here I am, at the end of my rope. It's the final act of a drama that's bombing and who walks through the door but the father of method acting."

Stanislavski didn't respond immediately, instead he patiently waited to see where the conversation would lead. It wound up at an unexpected destination.

"Listen, Constantin. I don't know much about you. Heck, I don't know how you got here or for that matter how your English improved so quickly, but I do know I want to hire you."

"Hire me?" Stanislavski was dumbfounded. "Hire me to do what?"

"Direct our marketing production."

"Marketing? I mean, I have some experience in that area, but nothing formal, just promoting my theater productions."

"In your thirty second elevator pitch for your acting method you've just told me more about marketing than the three people I've interviewed for the position! Here's what I heard: If you want to truly connect with customers as either an individual or an organization you first need to know yourself and what you can do well, then know your customer and their motivations before finally knowing how to effectively bring them together. If you can teach an actor and an acting company to do those three things, you probably can teach my company and my employees how to do it as well. *Who am I and what's my motivation here?* That's your line, isn't it? My employees need to learn how to think that way about our customers and our markets."

The CEO pushed back from his desk, crossed his legs and continued. "And, you know, it makes sense to me. There's a similarity. A theater company puts on a production. The director of the company assembles a cast, leads rehearsals, builds a set and directs other external elements such as music and lighting. But most importantly, the director is responsible for making sure the actors understand the material and the characters, and ultimately that the characters are portrayed in a way which tells the story and connects with the audience. When everything is in place, you present the performance to the audience in the hope that they will accept it, like it, connect with it and, I guess you could say, consume it."

He pulled the chair back up to his desk and leaned forward, addressing the next point directly to Stanislavski. "It's a bit different here at The Ater Company, but like you, we put on a production every day. My job is to assemble a cast that knows who we are and can decide which combinations of resources are going to be presented to our external audience. We need to determine how and where they will be presented and then present them on a regular basis in a way which will make consumers connect with them and want to accept them. And I want you to be part of the cast, Constantin. It may not be a lead part, but it's an awfully good supporting role."

Stanislavski chuckled at the theater reference and started to warm to the idea. "How does what I've said differ from what you've heard from the other candidates?" Stanislavski asked.

"I've gotten nothing but the academic definition from these people!" the CEO responded, the frustration evident in his voice. "I ask for vision, and I get sentences like, facilitating exchange relationships, descriptions of the four "P's" of product, price, promotion and placement. But that's all implementation, really. They talk distribution channels, getting things into stores, that sort of stuff. But they're usually talking about sales. What I need is someone who can think strategically and dynamically about the marketing and marketplace issues inherent in the marketing and selling processes. What I need is a way to *teach* our resources how to better connect with our markets and customers."

Stanislavski sat in amazement as the CEO began pacing energetically back and forth through the room pressing his points home with dramatic gestures aimed at his captive audience. "You see, when you focus only on implementation, all of your thinking and your planning becomes functional. Marketing gets separated out into compartments and it doesn't interact with the rest of the company. This is a pervasive problem right now here at The Atre Company. I have to tell you, old man Atre would be appalled if he were still around. All big companies have gone through their phases of mergers and acquisitions, downsizings, upsizings, and resizings. When companies are small, everyone has the same memories of the company and can recall similarly the company's experiences in the marketplace. We've gotten to the point where our singular collective experience has been lost because so many people have come and gone over the years. Over time that collective memory has become diluted by new and alternate experiences to the point where we no longer know ourselves as well as we did … or should. As a company and individuals we don't connect with our customers and we don't understand the relationship of the exchange. To compound matters, there's definitely no synthesis. Things here just aren't coming together like they should."

The CEO sat down on the corner of his desk and sighed. "My problem is that this is easy to say and hard as heck to teach. I have taught the concept from the business perspective but I guess in doing so I have been just like the people I criticize. I have relied on my business education and experience to teach my employees how to get to know the customer and how to better position this company in the market."

"Perhaps your problem is that very perspective," Stanislavski innocently interjected, his confidence beginning to reappear. "Perhaps it's your focus and reliance on business principles, taught in a business-like manner which is producing the results that you're unhappy with. When I teach actors to be characters, my approach is not to teach acting but to teach the principles of internal and external identification."

There was a long pause while Stanislavski's words sunk in with the CEO. "Now I really want to hire you," the CEO repeated, this time more firmly. "I think your ideas will be of use to this company, Constantin. I want you to apply the methods you've developed for a theater company and its actors to the people and problems we're experiencing in this company."

"Wait a second," Stanislavski cut in, "I don't know anything about marketing. I actually don't understand much of anything you've just said or that you've said I've said." Stanislavski shifted uncomfortably in his chair. "I don't even know what production you're doing here."

The CEO continued with what Stanislavski surmised was a natural confidence that had served him well in business. Stanislavski's conclusion that the confidence was natural was based on the fact that he could tell from experience that the CEO wasn't a very good actor. "Constantin, I'm not a man who takes no for an answer. And I'm not going to leave you hanging out there, waiting for you to fail. I'm not a method actor or director but I am a good manager and a good CEO. That means I know when to lead, when to do and when to delegate. Don't worry, I'm going to give you some very specific objectives, all based on the preliminary outline of the method that you've given me."

He walked over to a wooden cabinet on one of the walls in his office, opened the doors and revealed a whiteboard. Picking up one of the pens, he placed three bullets one on top of another, with enough space between each to add sentences later. "Consider this to be a contract between the two of us," the CEO said before he started writing, "assuming, of course, that you accept the assignment."

"First," he began, "the *internal* aspect of the acting method, namely understanding yourself and your capabilities as an actor. Teach our cast of characters how to better understand the core competencies and resources of this company and its employees, from a marketing perspective. There are two pieces to that: our marketing team needs to have a fundamental understanding of the business and the people who make it function. Collectively this is our *self*. They must be prepared to complement those capabilities and draw on each of them as needed given the demands of every scene they encounter."

The CEO filled in the first bullet with the words: ***understand the competencies and resources of the business self and understand how they can be applied when called upon***.

"Second," the CEO continued, "there is the *external* portion of the method. If memory serves, that involves understanding both the character you are going to play and the elements of portraying that particular character, right?"

"Absolutely," Stanislavski agreed.

"That portion of the method should help us get at the next point." The CEO turned and began writing again and filled in the second bullet: *Understand customers and stakeholders and identify the underlying motivations of their behaviors*. "You see," the CEO said, "I can commission whole mountains of market research, but that doesn't help me. I'm looking for a process that reinforces the need for customer focus, and I think your method might give us a way to truly understand our customers and ground that process."

"And then there's the third part, the *synthesis*." He turned back to the whiteboard and began writing on it again. As he spoke he wrote his third bullet which read: *Defining the implementation process for marketing and communications*. "This is taking your understanding of the business and the role of the marketing department, combining it with the understanding of the customer base, and mapping out a process that people can use after you're gone. It's the constitution for the marketing department and the company as a whole, if you will."

"Now, there's one thing I would caution you about, Constantin," the CEO said a bit grimly. "Many people get too caught up in the theory and not in the practice. I know you're not a marketing professional, but I can't have this process linger too long on the internal challenge. You have to get to the customer, the character of the customer, and you absolutely must get to synthesis. That's what we need to get our people thinking about."

The CEO walked away from the whiteboard and back over to where Stanislavski was sitting. "There are any number of consultants who could do this for me *by the book*, but the book is old and outdated. By that I mean the book's being read, not rewritten. I'm certainly not getting the performance I'm paying for." The CEO paused, pleased with his play on words. After a moment he continued. "So I'm willing to take a risk to see what you can do, but I don't have a lot of time. In three months, I need to show the board of directors some results and a vision for where this company can go. I am going to push you hard, meet with you on a regular basis, and see where you are in meeting this contract. What do you say?"

The CEO sat back down in his chair, pulled the cuffs on his shirt out a bit from his jacket, and waited for Stanislavski to agree to his proposal. He did not have to wait long.

"It sounds fascinating," Stanislavski responded and added half jokingly, "It's also a new role for me, and an old actor loves a new challenge." He thought about it for a few more seconds, and considered the objectives on the board. He really had no idea if he could actually do what the CEO had laid out, but he needed the job. Eventually, the idea of income overwhelmed his fear of the unknown road that lay ahead. He put on his brave face and said, "I'll accept your offer. I will play the part."

"I'm glad to hear that, Constantin. I'm looking forward to working with you." They both rose to shake hands from the opposite sides of the desk, and the CEO came around the side to place his hand on Stanislavski's shoulder. "But there's one other thing I would like to add to that list."

"Oh? What's that?"

"Something I referred to before," the CEO said. "The inside candidate I considered for the job, I want her to be able to take over where you leave off. Here's what I'd like to do. I will name you Marketing Director, with her as Assistant Director. I will put the two of you together and ask you, with the rest of your team, to produce a strategic marketing plan for our company. Over the next three months you will work with the cast in place. Use your method as the foundation for developing the plan. I'm not going to tell anyone who you really are until after the final presentation. I hope by then your assistant will be ready to take the position permanently. What do you think?"

"I always have been successful with young actors," Stanislavski responded with the confidence of a person committed to the task at hand. "I think I can be successful with younger marketing people as well."

"Great!" the CEO cheered in a highly controlled manner. "So, let's go meet her."

Before he could raise his voice to object, the CEO picked up his phone and asked his secretary to find out if the woman was in her office. "She's there," the answer came back on the intercom a few seconds later. The CEO got up, bowed dramatically and gestured toward the door. Once through he proceeded to guide Stanislavski down the hallway with his hand on Stanislavski's shoulder. When they stopped they were in front of two doors marked *Elevator*. Stanislavski wondered silently if he was expected to give that pitch the CEO had referred to back in his office once they were inside the elevator.

"Constantin," the CEO said as he pushed the button to call the elevator, "the woman to whom I'm introducing you is going to be a bit disappointed. She knows she's not getting the job, but the fact I've named someone to the position will come as a surprise to her. She'll resist some of your ideas at first but I am sure that in time you will win her over."

"Well, I hope so," Stanislavski replied, "or this is going to be a long three months."

Just before the doors to the elevator closed, the secretary called out and reminded the CEO that he would have a meeting in his office in fifteen minutes. "I'll be back," he said sounding annoyed at the prospect of having to cut short his excursion. "This won't take long."

"Just to remind you, Constantin," the CEO said, "I don't want people to even have a clue about your identity. But I know you're a great actor, so just follow my lead."

Before Stanislavski had a chance to ask what exactly he meant, the elevator doors opened to reveal a different floor and a thirty-something looking woman in a professional looking traditional blue business suit standing right in the doorway. But there was something a bit different in what she was wearing. Around her shoulder was a brightly colored, fashionable scarf that was perfectly matched with her neatly styled golden colored hair.

"Oh, here you are," the CEO exclaimed. Without pausing for a response, he continued, "This is Stan, Stan Islavski, our new Marketing Director."

After a beat of surprise, she held out her hand to greet him. He took her hand and smiled warmly in response without a moment's hesitation.

"Pleasure to meet you, Mr. Islavski."

"It's a pleasure to meet you as well, and please call me Stan." Stanislavski gave a quick glance in the CEO's direction and smiled. He made a mental note that he would have to talk to the CEO about his choice of names at some point in the future. In the meantime, "Stan" it was and he played along accordingly. "I have heard some wonderful things about your work," he said in an attempt to soften the harshness of the news that had just been delivered to his new supporting cast member.

"Thank you. Islavski, that's an interesting name. Where are you from?"

"Russia, actually. I was born there, but I left after...."

"The war, after the cold war," interjected the CEO a bit nervously. "He's been here for a while, and he has been a director for a number of production companies."

An awkward pause ensued as the three of them wondered who would speak next. The CEO glanced at his watch and said, "Well, I have to go, would you be so kind as to show Stan to his office? He'll be coming back tomorrow to start work. At least he should know where to show up. Oh, and you'll introduce him to everyone else tomorrow, won't you?"

"Certainly," the Assistant Director said with a noticeable mixture of disappointment and disapproval in her voice.

The CEO jumped back in the elevator and pressed the button.

"See you at rehearsal," Stanislavski said to the CEO as the elevator doors started to close. The last thing he saw before the doors closed completely was a confused look on the CEO's face.

Consumed by her disappointment the Assistant Director hadn't been paying attention and missed the comment completely. She turned awkwardly toward Stanislavski, put on a brave face and said, "I guess I'll show you to your office."

They walked down the hall without speaking. Stanislavski spoke first.

"You're angry, aren't you?"

She stopped and sized him up for a second. "No, I'm not angry."

"Are you sure?"

"Absolutely," she said after a pause. They continued down the hallway until they arrived at a corner office. "Well, here it is, Mr. Islavski, I mean, Stan," she said with a pleasant enough sounding tone. Her curt gesture, however, raised suspicion in Stanislavski that perhaps her motivation was other than befriending. "When you come in tomorrow, just stop at the receptionist desk and she'll let you in. We'll get you keys and..."

"Wait, wait a second." She stopped when Stanislavski interrupted her. "You are angry. You don't have to deny it. Your sentences are a bit clipped and I don't think that's your normal way of speaking. The splash of yellow around your shoulder shows you're not as stern as all that. I can see the motivation in your action. You wanted this job, and now you're meeting with someone you didn't even get a chance to speak with and assess before he was hired."

She was briefly startled by his candor and didn't have an immediate response. He extended his hand. "I'm looking forward to working with you. You must be a good marketing person or else you wouldn't be here. And you have more to teach me than you might surmise. For my part, I respect anyone who can control their emotions as well as you just did. You could easily pass for a good actress and, as you'll see, I have great respect for," he paused to pick the right words, "the performing arts."

She didn't have to tell him that he was right about her being angry. She simply smiled and shook his hand in a professional, business-like manner without revealing too much gratitude. "I'm looking forward to it, too. I will see you at nine o'clock tomorrow morning. The marketing department's senior staff will be ready for you."

She turned to leave the room and stopped just outside the doorway. "Oh, one more thing Stan …"

"Yes?"

"What shall I say the agenda is for the meeting tomorrow? Just the usual introductions?"

Stanislavski smiled. "Yes, but you can also tell them we'll be talking about how to be the person you are."

She smiled, thinking it a reference to the way she tried to hide her anger instead of as the next step on a road laid out for her by an actor and a seasoned business executive. As she left the office she couldn't help but think that despite her disappointment, it would be good to work with Stan, even if his clothes looked a bit wrinkled and clearly out of date.

* * * * * *

In his writings, Stanislavski outlined three challenges for the actor:

☐ *The internal challenge* — preparing for a role by getting to understand the person they are and how to "work on themselves" so they understand their own capabilities as an actor;

☐ *The external challenge* — building a character through movement, diction, expression and control;

☐ *The synthesis of internal and external* — creating a role which reflects the "truth" of acting.

Stanislavski and the CEO have just rewritten those challenges and made them applicable to the marketing function by defining them as follows:

☐ *The internal challenge* — preparing to play a role in the marketplace by understanding the inner resources and capabilities of the company and its people;

☐ *The external challenge* — understanding the "character of the customer" in terms of their motivations, perspective on the world and specific purchasing behaviors; and,

☐ *The synthesis* — creating effective products, service offerings and communications that bring together internal capabilities and a demonstrated understanding of the character of the customer.

The basic concepts of marketing are wrapped up in these three elements. Price, for instance, is:

☐ an internal challenge — what are we capable of producing and at what value can we produce our products?

☐ an external challenge — how does a particular customer evaluate value with respect to a given product at a given moment?

☐ a matter of synthesis — how do we deliver our product in a manner that connects with the value perceptions and consumption motivations of our customers?

You can think about almost any major corporate product development or communications challenge using the three elements Stanislavski outlined in his method. You might, before flipping to the next chapter, try a few more that you're struggling with right now, just to get used to thinking about challenges and techniques in this fashion.

In each of the upcoming chapters, we'll be giving you more specific questions to think about and ideas to consider as you apply Stanislavski's method to your specific interests and situations. For now, we invite you to turn the page and find out how Stan does in his first day on the job.

Scene II

Work on One's Self

Know what has come before

Have you ever been in a meeting where the topic of conversation revolves around what should be done without considering what has been done, why its been done and what it implies for what can be done? The next scene in our story shows how Stan handles this on his first day at work.

* * * * * * * *

From the moment he entered the room, four sets of eyes were trained on Stanislavski. The first pair belonged to the Assistant Director, who rose to greet him and began the formal introduction process. He met the Product Manager, who was responsible for all of the different items made and sold by The Ater Company, and then the Communications Manager, who had a portfolio of all of the advertising and public relations materials related to the products and services of The Ater Company. Finally, there was the Research Manager, who informed Stan that he had come prepared with something he referred to as a *powerpoint* on his laptop. Stanislavski hid his confusion at what he had just been told, as the fellow seemed very anxious to show the thing to the new Director.

Stanislavski was relieved when he learned that in fact, the Research Manager's reference was to a portable computer, which was connected to a projection device of some sort. No sooner had the initial introductions been completed, when the Research Manager pressed a button and colorful charts were projected onto the wall at the front of the room.

"This is an interesting looking ... projection," he said, a bit confused by all the colorful charts and fancy three-dimensional graphics displayed.

"Yes, that represents the core of our market research over the past six months, and, if we skip to slide thirty-seven, there's something I would like to show you ..."

"Come on, now," the Product Manager interrupted, "we don't want to bore him to death on his very first day."

"...but it says a lot about our customer base..."

"Our quickly shrinking customer base," quipped the Communications Manager.

"... and what their expectations are for our products, which are ..."

Stanislavski leaned forward and placed both of his hands palm down on the table in a dramatic gesture that communicated authority. The movement caused the Research Manager to stop his unsolicited presentation. Stanislavski looked around the room at each of the three managers. He turned to the Assistant Director and asked, "What is this company, and who are each of you?"

"The Ater Company," she responded immediately.

"Not the name of the company, the *self* of the company. What is this company?"

All of the faces in the room were blank, except for the Assistant Director. After a brief pause, she ventured a guess.

"I guess that depends on who you ask. I mean if you get input from our HR people, it's the employees that make up the company. If you get input from the IT people, it's the network, the servers, the backbone and the infrastructure. If you get input from the finance people, it's our asset base, our inventory, our equipment, the physical plant, you know, that kind of stuff. Our sales people say it's the distribution channels ..."

"Hold on," Stanislavski interrupted, "I'm asking you, not those people."

Flustered, and not knowing what he was looking for, she shrugged and said, "I would say it's the quality of our product line, our reputation with customers, and our ongoing relationship with the market."

Stanislavski shook his head. He leaned back on his chair and said, "I have worked with a number of companies, but none, I must admit, quite like this. It is important to understand that within each company there are key..." he paused momentarily to choose the right term so that he could stay in character, "there are key players, and there are supporting players. No production can occur without the combined contribution of all the players, but, to understand the kind of production we can undertake, we have to know who and what the players are, as people, as *self*. So, as a Director, I always begin working on the *self* before we spend talking about our production."

Stan looked around for a moment, concerned that he had just blown his cover. He stopped, shifted again, and realized that no one had made the connection. Interesting, he usually didn't have any trouble staying in character. Maybe he just needed to apply the method to himself a bit better, he thought. He took a moment with his thoughts while he reconnected himself with *Stan*, his current role.

"In this circumstance," Stanislavski continued, "we have been charged with the task of reconnecting this company with its audience, or as we say in marketing, the customer and the market. But to do that we first have to connect with our self."

None of the managers knew how to respond. It certainly wasn't the kind of comment that they expected of a Marketing Director. Recognizing their confusion, Stanislavski continued, "Trust me, there is a method to my madness, as you will see. We've only got three months to produce a new marketing plan, a script if you will, for this company." The managers were staring at him curiously. "We need to take a good hard look at ourselves if it is going to get done," he continued. "We need to get to know the company we are, the company 'self', before we start talking about the markets we can serve. Only then can we draw from our resources to connect our capabilities with the expectations and requirements of the characters and the audience."

"I think you mean customers," the Assistant Director said.

"Actually, he's right. Our customers sure are characters," quipped the Product Manager.

Everyone laughed while Stanislavski righted himself. "Customers ... yes, customers."

"Are you asking us why we work here?" interjected the Product Manager.

"No, not exactly," he replied. "What I want to know is what each player in the company brings with himself to their role."

"Or *her* self," added the Assistant Director with a hint of contempt over the apparently sexist remark.

"Yes, you are correct," Stanislavski agreed. "I am also looking to expand our knowledge about the company we are, and work on what you might call our business self. Where have we been? What experiences do we have to draw on? What does each of us contribute to the whole? What are we good at? What are we bad at? What kind of roles should we be ready to play? When I refer to 'we' I mean both us as individuals and the company as a collective individual. What is our range? I want us to inventory our collective experiences and knowledge, and use that introspection to broaden our corporate self."

The Research Manager tentatively raised his hand, and, after waiting a moment for a recognition that did not formally come, decided to add his comments unsolicited. "This doesn't seem to have to do with the customers, or the research I have here."

Stanislavski interrupted him. "That's important, and we'll get to that. But that's the dialog. We can't begin our work on dialog until we have worked on our self. Here, I'll give you an analogy," he continued. "An intelligent man I know very well once wrote that *the person you are is ten times more interesting than the player you can be.* This wise man said," he continued, quoting his own work, "*you start with who you are and you act who you are, because faking it just doesn't work, it's just not interesting. First and foremost, that means getting to know what you are capable of.*" He was changing some of the acting references as he quoted his own writings in an effort to stay in character. It seemed to be working.

"If you're very flexible, you can play the role of an acrobat," he continued, "but, if you're more portly, you likely can't, unless you do a lot of stretching exercises. If you're a man, you'll have some difficulty playing a woman."

"Unless you get surgery," quipped the Product Manager, evoking smiles across the room.

"Exactly. Now, as I understand it, this company, this collective individual as I called it, has the same sort of problem. The company doesn't seem to connect with its audience of customers. That might be because we don't have a clear picture of who we are, both as individuals within this production company or as a collective self."

"To be fair," the Assistant Director responded, "we do have lines of business, individual profit centers, and a written statement of core competencies."

"Let's forget them for a moment," Stanislavski said with a wave of his hand, "even though they might be what I'm looking for. If we start from scratch we first need to understand what makes up the self. If, as I understand it, our job is to truly connect with our customers, then our first job is to collect the knowledge of the self. So, what can we do to work on our individual and collective self?"

At this point the Assistant Director turned to Stan and asked, "But what is the self we are seeking?" She wasn't sure exactly where this was leading but she felt emboldened by her apparent grasp of the theory. She continued her question, "Is it us as individuals, or is it the company as a whole?"

"I've always thought we were a bit schizophrenic here. Maybe we have multiple selves too," joked the Product Manager.

Stan paused to think about her question. It was a good one. He hadn't been prepared to be challenged about the application of his method at such an early stage in the process and he wasn't exactly sure how to answer. One thing he knew, however, was that he needed to preserve an image of authority and confidence. "I think we'll have to answer that one together," he replied. "Perhaps we have many personalities and many selves, but I believe that in the end there will be a collective self that we will identify and work on."

"Maybe we should do a survey or audit of some sort," suggested the Research Manager.

The Communications Manager grimaced. "Not another marketing audit!"

"No, I don't think that's what I mean," the Research Manager replied. "I'm talking about something like an audit of our self, a self audit."

"Wait a minute," she said to no one in particular. "That might not be such a bad idea." The Assistant Director was thinking aloud. "Stan is saying we need get a better handle on the company's self. Is there a better way to begin then by asking people," she paused, "and departments for that matter, what they have done, what they currently do, what they think that the rest of us do, and what they think they're capable of doing? You know, who we are?" She still wasn't quite sure where she was going with this line of thinking but she felt like she was on a roll so she barreled forward. "Maybe the idea of truly canvassing our 'self' rather than just the standard 'what do you think we should do' survey will actually lead somewhere."

"What are we waiting for, then?" Stan asked enthusiastically. "Let's begin the process. Who would you like to talk to first? Who do we know the least about and what part of our self are we least in touch with?"

"I'd like to talk to Sales and Distribution," answered the Communications Manager.

"I'd like to take you to R&D, you know Research and Development," answered the Research Manager.

"Finance," the Assistant Director said. "We should go there first. They're the ones pushing the new pricing based solely on absolute unit margins. They don't see that we can't differentiate ourselves given their cost structure, which I think is artificially driven by targeted profit margins and earnings forecasts. It seems backwards to me, but I'm just me, not them. There must be a motivation there but I'm not getting it." She thought about it for a moment. With an uncertain expression and tone of controlled confidence in her voice she said, "I don't understand that part of our self."

The question made Stanislavski optimistic, giving him a hint that the woman he was teaching was starting to get the point. "Lead the way." Stanislavski gestured and allowed the Assistant Director to lead him down the hallway. Behind him, he heard the Communications Manager whisper to the Product Manager, "great, our first meeting's gone mobile. You bring your new tablet?"

Stanislavski was about to ask what a tablet was, but before he could look over his shoulder and pose the question, the group turned the corner and walked straight into an office. The door proclaimed the name and title of the occupant — Chief Financial Officer.

"The inquisition has arrived," he sighed, taking off his glasses and throwing them on the desk. "I guess you're all here to talk about the dismal returns created by your pricing plans. You'd have to sell a boat load of product to make that pricing compelling to my constituents."

"Actually, I don't know the first thing about this ... pricing strategy," Stan smiled, "but that's not the kind of proposal we were thinking about."

The CFO focused on Stan's face and realized that he did not know this new person. The Assistant Director awkwardly raised her eyebrows and started the introduction, "I am sorry, I thought you two would have met earlier as part of the interview process. This is Stan Islavski, our new Director."

The CFO stood up and extended his hand. "Stan, good to meet you. I didn't know that they had filled the position. I have to say, this comes as a bit of a surprise." He looked over at the Assistant Director suspiciously but aimed his question at Stan. "Why haven't they explained the pricing strategy proposal to you yet?"

"I haven't asked for it, at least not yet. Do you mind if I take a seat for a moment?"

"Well, I don't think I have enough chairs for all of you."

"This won't take long, and I'm not sitting down to get comfortable. I'd just like to write down your responses to a few of the questions I have asked of my team."

"Which are?"

"We are on a mission to identify and work on the self of The Ater Company. So first I would like you to tell us about the self of the Finance department."

A confused CFO sat silently in his chair wondering what he was being asked to identify. "I'm not sure what you're looking for," he responded slowly.

"As the marketing group here, we are charged with the task of connecting this company and its products with customers acting in the theater of the marketplace. In order to make that connection, we have to be able to get into character so we've determined that we must first work to know our *self* so that we know who we are and what internal resources we have to work with."

The CFO finally had something to latch onto. "I see, you're interested in internal resources. You want me to tell you about our fixed asset base, our access to and cost of capital, our soft costs - both fixed and variable, things like that, right?"

It was as if the CFO began speaking Portuguese. Russian, he understood. Finance was a language lost on him.

The Assistant Director, recognizing Stanislavski's pause, tried to help. "No, I don't think that is what we're after. I think," as she continued she turned slightly toward Stanislavski in a gesture of insecurity, "and correct me if I'm wrong Stan, we are looking for what experiences, capabilities, knowledge, and," she paused again as she tried to recall the term Stan had used earlier, "and *range* that you as an individual, and your department as a collective, contribute to our *self*." With a reassuring nod from Stan she turned back to the CFO. "We are on a quest to identify who we are as a company so we can inventory the range of assets we bring to bear in making marketplace decisions." She looked over at Stan who offered her a smile in acknowledgement of her effort.

For the next few minutes, the CFO talked to the marketing team about his experiences. He had been with The Ater Company for over fifteen years so he had many stories to tell about stages in the company's development cycles. He talked about his development and about the development of the finance department. He complained about changes in GAAP accounting procedures over recent years. He told them how the banks and vendors had reacted to different capitalization strategies the company had employed and finally he bragged unabashedly about how the company had generated and delivered returns to its shareholders.

Toward the end of his dissertation, he talked about his changing role at the company over time. In recent years, he told the group, he had become less of an accountant and more of a salesman. His customers were not the customers of the company, he told the group, but rather the financial constituents of the company. His products were not the products of the company, but rather his product was the company itself. As he spoke, he began to realize that he, too, needed to find the self of the company so that he could better connect his product with, as they had put it, the character of *his* customers.

Stanislavski listened closely, writing down key phrases and ideas. After a few minutes, a pause in the narrative presented itself and Stanislavski decided to reclaim control of the conversation by asking a different sort of question. "Now, how would you describe Distribution and Sales?"

The CFO chuckled. "Too expensive and not enough, respectively."

"Ok, but what do you know about them and how do they contribute to our self? What experiences do they have that add to the resources and range of the company?"

Secure with the term resources again, the CFO gave the laundry list of resources of Distribution followed closely by Sales. Stanislavski let him go briefly and then interrupted, "No, I'm not looking for their asset base as you call it, I'm looking for what they bring to the collective self. For instance," Stanislavski flipped back through his notes, "you talked about the principles of financial controls. And you mentioned something, you called it *socks*, after which the principles changed for the department. Your contribution to the 'self' became different, didn't it? Have there been events like that at Distribution that you would characterize it as part of the 'self' we're looking for?"

Beginning to understand Stan's point, and realizing that he was unsure of the answer, the CFO simply shrugged. "If you're talking about Sarbanes Oxley you're right, that really made me question *my* self." He figured he was the only one that got the play on words but that was alright with him. He got the joke and sometimes that was enough.

"We're going there next," Stan said as he began to put his papers away. Suddenly the CFO stood and put on his coat. "Do you have a meeting to get to?" Stan asked, surprised by the sudden gesture.

"Sure do," replied the CFO, "I'm going to Distribution and Sales with you. I'm curious about this *self* you keep talking about and I want to know what they contribute to it. "

"Let's be off then," added the Assistant Director.

"Yeah, we'll just follow the yellow brick road, Dorothy," mumbled the Communications Manager under her breath. She turned deliberately to the Research Manager, put her hand on his shoulder and said, "Come on Scarecrow."

The group laughed and headed off to Distribution and Sales. As they walked, the CFO turned to Stan, "You play golf, Stan? If you play, we could include you in our next corporate event."

"Oh," Stanislavski smiled, "there's very little I can't play, when I put my mind to it."

"Good, we'll have to have you out at some point."

They entered the elevator and began to descend to a lower floor. The bell rang and the group moved out into the hallway and followed the arrow which pointed to "Distribution."

Opening the door, they were greeted with the sight of dozens of cubicles, with people moving hurriedly from cubicle to cubicle. Stanislavski thought they looked a bit frantic and unchoreographed. He thought to himself that some of the gestures were a bit wild, but, since the pace of the whole place was significantly faster than those he was used to, he didn't make that much of it until the Product Manager commented under his breath. "Chaos, that's their contribution to the self."

Stanislavski paused to observe the scene and began to see the pattern. People from sales were clamoring over to the people in distribution, asking questions, looking frustrated and ultimately returning to their offices. People from distribution were getting up with information in hand, walking over to sales, and getting into arguments.

"So, you wanted to speak with the person in charge of distribution. Their director is right over here," indicated the Product Manager as they went around another corner and knocked on a half open door.

"What is it? Can I help you?"

The Product Manager pushed open the door and, with an ingratiating smile and inviting tone of voice said, "Do you have a second? I wanted to introduce you to our new Director, Stan Islavski."

The Distribution Manager rose, revealing a heavy set frame, a coffee stained shirt and tie that didn't quite match his outfit. As he moved around his desk Stanislavski said, "And I'm sure you know our friend here," gesturing to the CFO.

"Sure, good to see you although I must admit I'm surprised to see you here. I've got a few minutes, but things are a bit chaotic around here, as you can see. I've got a report due tomorrow to the COO, I've got to explain why we don't seem to be able to connect with sales and get all of the products to the right place at the right time." Looking at the CFO he added, "Or cost effectively, right?" The CFO nodded in agreement.

"I must admit," he continued, "I feel like I've been through this song and dance routine a few times before."

Stanislavski was a bit confused by the use of this term 'COO'. He tried to pronounce it in his mind, "coo?" "so?" Then his mind wandered back to the organizational chart that the CEO had left on his desk that morning and recalled *Chief Operating Officer*. He directed his attention to the Distribution Manager and said, "We don't want to take up much of your time. I'm just getting oriented to our corporate self."

"Well, you've come to the center of disorientation, and I have no idea what you mean by corporate self," the Distribution Manager replied, fumbling through some papers. "Go ahead, ask away."

With a bit of an edge in her voice, the Assistant Director asked, "What are your resources and what is your range? What can you do here in Distribution? Not what do you do, what can you do both as individuals and as a collective?"

The Distribution Manager stopped what he was doing. After that question, the group had his undivided attention.

As he looked around for clarification, the CFO added a comment. "They were just in my office and they asked me the same question. I answered it as best I could by telling them about the experiences we have had in finance and what I think we as a company can draw from them. But then he asked me about you. I couldn't answer, so I came along."

"So, you don't know what we do?"

"I know what you do," the CFO responded, "but I've got to admit, I know a lot less about what you have done and can do."

The Assistant Director continued the line of questioning. "So, tell us a bit about you and your cast of characters. How do you contribute to our corporate self?" She was proud of herself for her extension of the analogy.

The Distribution Manager smiled and was suddenly more animated. "I can answer the question pretty easily. All I have to do is take you over to our flowchart here and I'll give you the whole orientation ..."

Stopping him before he could drown them all in too much detail, the Assistant Director cut him off by saying, "I don't think you need to get that deep just yet. Just tell us about your self and the department's self."

For the next few minutes the Distribution Manager did just that. He talked about the approaches they had tried and the successes (and failures) associated with them. He focused on how his job had changed with the advent of the Internet, on-line tracking processes and the new just-in-time delivery system for the company he rolled out a few years back. He chronicled how, when he was a line supervisor out at one of the distribution centers, it took them a whole week to figure out where a shipment of product had wound up, because no one had bothered to work through all of the screens that came with what he referred to as *that crazy software the company had implemented.*

As his monologue drew to a close he reflected on his childhood when he helped his father with his Ham radio set-up in their garage. He remarked that his father would tell him that radio communications had changed the world. Now he was implementing an RFID (radio frequency identification device) system for tracking the company's inventory.

"I guess dad was right," he said as if to nobody in particular. The obvious nostalgia seemed out of character but also gave the others an insight into his self.

Throughout the conversation, Stanislavski took his notes and listened attentively while his staff asked more questions about the resources and capabilities of the distribution department. He waited for a pause, and then redirected the conversation again.

"We don't want to take up too much of your time. You have to prepare for your presentation and I know how important it is to prepare for being in the spotlight."

"Yeah, it's the old dog and pony show," the Distribution Manager smiled.

Stanislavski thought to himself that he wasn't familiar with that show and made a mental note to look it up when he returned to his extensive private library. "Let me ask you one more question." Stanislavski flipped back through his notes to the page where he wrote down the other departments mentioned by his staff. "Can you tell me about the *self* which my colleagues here called, wait a minute, what did they call it, R&D?"

"Research and Development? I know a bit about what they do, pretty technical stuff though." The Distribution Manager paused for a second, scratched his head and said, "But, you know, I don't think I've ever met anyone from over there. We don't really have much in common, Distribution and R&D."

"That's precisely the issue." Stanislavski was standing now, pacing around the office. "You are both parts of the same self we are working on. Both of your work is critical in the definition of our corporate self."

"We're talking to them next," the Assistant Director said. "Would you like to join us?"

"Sounds a lot more interesting than the presentation," the Distribution Manager replied.

With one more person added to the conversation, the group prepared to move on. Stanislavski turned to the Assistant Director and asked, "Do you see where this is taking us?"

"Yes, I think I do," she responded. "We're beginning to get a pretty complete map of all of the experiences and ranges of this company. We can put them together; maybe we can do some sort of formal inventory. That will give us a better sense of what the collective *self* of this company is. How we perceive ourselves as different from other companies, questions about what we do and how we do it. I don't think we've done anything like that around here for a long time."

"Wait a second," the Communications Manager jumped in. "Is that really our job? I mean, we're a marketing department, we're not HR."

"But this is a different sort of exercise," the Assistant Director countered. "We're not looking for employee attitudes here; we're looking for something more fundamental. We should probably go over to HR and talk it over with them and get to know their range."

"Any director of a production company," Stanislavski began slowly, "needs to be sure that each member of his cast knows their *self*, and he needs to know the capabilities and inner resources of each of the members of his or her company. And, he needs to be sure that the cast of characters, as you put it," he gave a quick smile to the Research Manager who had used the term earlier, "is cast correctly," he concluded. "That is a director's job."

The same scene repeated itself in R&D. A confused manager, the clarification, the help from the other managers and then off to the next department. By the end of the day, Stanislavski peeled off from the group, which had grown, then broken apart into two, then three groups, all talking with each other, planning visits to other departments and other offices. He returned to his office, leaving a frenzy of activity in his wake that would lead his team to a better sense of the 'self' of The Ater Company.

* * * * * *

"The person you are is a thousand times more interesting than the best actor you could ever hope to be."

When Stanislavski made that comment in the course of his writings about the Method, he meant to emphasize what he calls "working on the self." Understanding who you are, and working to expand who you are, is the first step in becoming the actor you can be.

As the great actor, director and Professor at the Yale Drama School Robert Lewis put it in his celebrated lecture series on Stanislavski's method:

"... you should work to enlarge your knowledge of the world, the people in it, and their characters and relationships. Also, you should sharpen your observance of situations on life, develop your imagination and

sensitivity, because those are the things which you store up to feed you in whatever you do in your work ... 'work on one's self' is so basic that it is the foundation of the whole edifice."

One of the primary objectives of marketing is connecting the capabilities and outputs of a company with the expectations and demands of the marketplace. Before you can go out and connect either the company or yourself with the customer, however, you must first develop knowledge of both your *self* and of the company *self*. Then you can find out where work needs to be done to expand the experience of both *selves*.

In that regard, the Stanislavski Method offers perhaps the best starting place for connecting with customers and the marketplace. According to the Method, it all begins with generating an appropriate definition of what the individuals and company can really deliver.

So, how does a company "work on one's self?" Simple. You begin with where and what you are.

The corporate *self* is a combination of the individual *selves* within the company; individual people, departments, profit centers, customer service teams, physical plant, etc. The marketer begins by getting to know the individual selves (including the *self* that is marketing) of the various resources within the company that comprise the whole. Only then, when the work on understanding the self has begun, can the marketer hope to expand the basic knowledge and experience of the corporate organization to better connect the corporate *self* to the consumer.

In an ideal world, the best way to understand the self is to do what Stanislavski and his team did, begin an internal conversation about who and what the company is. You probably won't have time to talk to everybody, but consider some of these situations:

Think about the last time you walked through a major corporate office. When you looked at the signs for various departments, did you know what the responsibilities of each department were? If you are thinking about a company where you work, do you know at least one person in each of those departments you could call on to find out what they do?

The first step in the process is developing an understanding of what information about the *self* you have access to and what information you'll need to acquire through research and discussion. If your network is not broad enough to reach throughout an organization, it will be difficult to do any effective marketing because you won't know the range of resources your company has at its disposal as you formulate a strategy for connecting with the customers and markets you are trying to reach.

Think about how you presently find out about the corporate or institutional *self* where you are working. How do you receive that information? Conversations? Newsletters and pieces of paper? The Internet, e-mail? What have you seen with your own eyes, heard with your own ears? What comes to you second or third hand about your corporate "self?"

People connect with the corporate or institutional *self* in many ways. One such way is through communication. Understanding what the forms of communication are and how you access them best is a critical part of identifying the *self*, and, as we will see in later chapters, using internal communications channels to help expand the *self* to meet the needs and interests of customers.

But neither an actor nor a corporation can permit themselves to get lost in the self for too long. For Stanislavski, they are connected to a central concept: **Action.**

Scene III

Action

Actions really do speak louder than words

It is often said that actions speak louder than words. In the next scene, Stanislavski teaches his team what that concept means for an actor and how a company should define action in terms of positioning itself, its products and its services in the marketplace.

* * * * * * * *

A few days later, Stanislavski convened the marketing team to talk about their progress. His hand written invitation had only indicated that it was time to apply the work they had been doing on the self. The expectation was that they would talk about their individual conversations and what they had learned about the corporate *self*, so each of them prepared a few notes (or, in the case of the Research Manager, a few dozen slides) that they could use. Instead, when they showed up with lattes and coffees in hand to start the meeting, they were confronted by a large sign sitting in the center of the table. One word was written on the sign.

ACTION

Stanislavski sat coyly on the far side of the table as each individual of the group sat down. It immediately became clear to all of them that this was to be a meeting with a very different agenda than expected.

"Where are the lights and camera?" joked the Research Manager, his face not hiding the disappointment he felt as he realized that once again his new boss would not be interested in his charts and graphs.

"Finding out who we are is all very well and good," Stanislavski began with a bit of a flourish, "but the *self* is made to act."

Stanislavski leaned across the table and gestured in the direction of the Communications Manager. "What are you doing right now," he asked abruptly.

"I'm sitting in a meeting with the marketing team," she replied.

"Ah, but what are you doing in the meeting?"

"I guess right now I'm answering a question."

"That's not an action," responded Stanislavski. "At least not for me."

"Of course that's an action," countered the Communications Manager. "It's what I'm doing."

"It may be what you are doing, but it is not what I would define as your action. Tell me, why are you answering the question?"

"Because you asked me the question."

"But why did you respond? There are a number of potential reasons. For instance, one reason may be that you like me and you wanted to be civil, so you answered the question. On the other hand, perhaps you hate me and you wanted to get back at me for something I did in the past, so you answered the question. Or, there's also the fact that I'm your boss and you feel that you have to answer the question, so you answered the question even though you thought it was a stupid question."

"Stan," the Assistant Direction interrupted, "I think we understand your point, but why is this important? We came prepared to talk about the work we're doing to understand our corporate self and now we're talking about something completely different. You sure are a character, Stan."

Stan smiled inexplicably. She had no idea of the compliment she had just paid him.

"I had prepared several slides on our self for a presentation," the Research Manager complained.

"Working on the self is something you always do so I'm thrilled that you've started the process; self is always a part of the discussion so it's good that you came prepared. But what I'm doing is moving forward. What I'm getting at now is very important to us because unless we tie our work on the corporate self to action, we'll never really be able to act."

"And that means we'll never get our customers back," the Product Manager agreed, "because we'll be too busy sitting around, staring at our corporate selves in the mirror."

"But I just told you what I was doing," the Communications Manager said. "I am answering a question. That's an action, isn't it?"

"Its part of one," Stanislavski responded, "but it's not a complete answer. An action is fundamentally tied to a motivation. Why am I doing what I do?" Putting on his best air of nonchalance, he continued, "I'm sure you've heard actors asking, *what's my motivation here?*" He looked around to see if he'd aroused any suspicion. He hadn't. "I'm not just sitting down on a bench, there is a specific reason I'm sitting down on a bench. Maybe I'm tired and I am sitting *to rest my legs after a long walk.* Maybe someone is pointing a gun at me and I am sitting to *comply with a person's demand.* Sitting on a bench is not an action without motivation.*"*

"So the School House Rock people were wrong," mumbled the Research Manager.

"What?" The incredulity of the Communications Manager spread to the others in the room. "What are you talking about?"

After an embarrassing pause, the Research Manager blurted out, "you remember the music, you know, from the Saturday morning cartoon shows? They had one song, went something like..." he paused to clear his throat and warbled out, "Verb! That's what's happening!"

"Don't quit your day job," the Product Manager said, giving the Research Manager a friendly pat on the back as a show of support.

"No, I'm serious! The examples you just used Stan, they aren't just verbs. It's not just "answering" something or "sitting down" on something. What's happening is the whole scene, the whole picture."

"I take that back," the Product Manager commented. "Maybe you should quit your day job. You can't sing, but you can make some money interpreting songs."

53

"I've never heard the song," Stanislavski said, taking control of the conversation again, "but you're right. Describing an action correctly, any action including the purchase of a product, requires more than a verb, it requires a whole phrase that integrates the motivation."

Stanislavski reached down below the table and pulled out another cue card with four bullets written on it. The handwriting was messy but it was legible. It read:

Describing an Action – The Stan Way

- Physically capable of being done

- Specific

- Not an errand

- Does not presuppose any physical or emotional state

"Sooner or later, Stan, I'll expect you to explain the relevance of this," the Assistant Manager said after reading the sign. "For now, I'll bite. What do you mean by each of these?"

He smiled. "I'm glad you asked that."

"The first criterion of an action is straightforward enough," Stanislavski began. **"If it can't be done, it's not an action you can do."**

"So, jumping over the moon, that doesn't work," the Communications Manager said.

"Unless you're a cow," joked the Product Manager.

"The second criterion is perhaps the most important," Stanislavski continued. "To describe an action appropriately, **it has to be specific**. That was my point," Stanislavski turned to the Communications Manager, "in my response to your response. 'Answering a question' is not very specific. In fact, it's downright generic. It's something that could be done by anyone, any time, anyplace."

The Assistant Director moved to ask a question. "What you're asking for in describing an action, then, is specific place and time and background."

"Not exactly," responded Stanislavski, "More like a specific motivation, a specific reason that connects the action to the self."

"Which is why we need to start with the *self*," the Assistant Director said, thinking out loud. "Or else we'd never know what we we're really doing."

Stanislavski smiled and continued through his four bullet points. "The third element is that **it cannot be an errand**. It can not be something you do for the sake of doing."

"Like, going to the corner store and getting some milk," the Communications Manager proposed.

"Why are you getting the milk?"

She considered it for a moment. "For my children, let's say."

"That's not a motivation. Why would you get milk for your children?"

"Because they want it for their cereal in the morning?"

"More fundamental," Stanislavski pushed her. "What is the nature of your relationship to your children?"

"I'm their mother."

"And how does that motivate you to do things for them?"

She thought about it for a minute. "I am getting milk both *to provide a healthy drinking alternative for my children.*"

"Good," Stanislavski commented in response. "That's good."

"But sometimes I have a different motivation," she added. "Sometimes I go to the store to get milk *to get out of the house to have a few minutes alone in peace and quiet.* Sometimes we don't need milk but I go to the store to get some anyway."

"That's good as well," Stanislavski added. "It shows that one action can have two entirely separate motivations."

"What about that last one?" the Research Manager asked. "**An action must not presuppose any physical or emotional state.**"

Stanislavski rose from his chair and walked over to the door. "I am leaving the room *to get something to quench my thirst!*" He walked out of the room, into the corridor and paused for a moment. "I am entering the room in order *to continue my explanation!*" The second announcement was followed by Stanislavski's reappearance.

A dramatic bow by Stanislavski in jest was followed by a smattering of applause, started by the Production Manager. Then Stanislavski shut the door, walked to the opposite side of the room, and announced, "I am *leaving the room to quench my thirst!*" He walked face first into the wall opposite the door and successfully executed a first-rate prat fall that had everyone around the table jumping up to come to his aid.

"I'm fine, I'm fine," Stanislavski said as he rose to his feet. "I've done that sort of thing more times than you'd imagine." People returned to their seats, and Stanislavski continued to make his point. "I did it on purpose. Pretend the door didn't exist and all of the walls were like the one I walked into. I could not go in the other room to quench my thirst if no door existed so that is not an action. It presupposes a physical condition: namely, an exit."

He sat back down in his chair and said, "Now we can get down to business."

Suspecting that Stan didn't really mean it when he said *business*, each person in the room silently wondered the same question. It was Stan's second week and they had yet to talk about the business of The Ater Company. As they wondered individually and collectively about where he was heading they braced themselves for another barrage of questions.

"What are we, as a company, doing right now? What are our *actions*?"

He paused, and followed up his own question with another question. "After that, tell me what our customers are doing right now? What *actions* is the marketplace taking as we sit here?. What actions are our customers taking when they buy our products?"

He looked around the room like a teacher in a classroom of bright students, each looking a bit stumped, trying to beat the other to an answer and approval. The Assistant Director gave the first effort.

"I'll start with us. How about, we are competing in the marketplace with our products?"

Stanislavski shook his head. "That's not specific. You must connect it to a motivation."

The Communications Manager tried to build on that beginning. "Competing in the marketplace to become the market leader."

Again, Stanislavski shook his head, but this time it was because he didn't understand the second phrase. "To be the market leader? What is that?"

"That's how we describe our strategy," the Assistant Director explained. "We want to be the market leader, you know, have the biggest market share."

"Is that specific?"

All of them thought in silence for a moment. The Product Manager ventured a possibility. "There's a specific market we serve. Specific competitors..."

"That's a crock of," the Assistant Director stopped herself and allowed her voice to trail off so she wouldn't complete the sentence. "People don't just choose to purchase *our* products as opposed to those of our direct competitors, we know that. They choose from a variety of purchasing options including no purchase at all. There's a variety of products and services they could buy out there and we're not just competing with competitors, we're chasing the value and purchasing power of customers. And, on top of that, what about new product and services that don't even have a market yet, much less a market leader!"

"I guess we really don't even know if being a market leader is even physically capable of being done," added the Communications Manager. "Even if we knew the exact value of the market at any given time and the total sales of every piece of everything, we might not have the production capability, for instance."

"Clearly," Stanislavski said, "we have to find a better way to describe our strategy. But we can save that for another time. Let's start over again, but first, take a look through the notes you brought. Think of what you saw happening, of the individual pieces of the corporate *self* that you've been looking at. What are we, as a company, doing right now?"

The Research Manager flipped through his slides, pulling out the one summarizing the conversation with the CFO. "We're changing our pricing strategy."

"Not yet, we're not," the Assistant Director said a bit combatively.

"Maybe not," Stanislavski responded, "but let's go with that one, in theory." He shook his head, a gesture the team was becoming all too familiar with. "That's still not specific."

The Research Manager thought for a moment, and offered: "Changing our pricing strategy to improve our profit margins."

"That presumes a physical state," the Product Manager said. "It presumes that other costs, such as distribution and sales overhead, aren't raised at the same time. That would cut into the improved profit margins."

"Changing our pricing strategy, making our customers happy," the Communications Manager suggested.

"Presupposes an emotional state on the part of our customers," responded the Product Manager. "How do you know they're unhappy about our pricing strategy?"

The Assistant Director leaned across the table to Stanislavski and said, *"Attempting to get what we think we deserve for the value of our product or, in other words, validating our effort with commensurate reward."*

They all sat for a moment to see if anyone could poke a hole in that construction. Stanislavski raised his coffee mug in a congratulatory gesture, saying "you've won the prize!"

After taking a sip, he continued the conversation. "We've just gone through an important exercise, though it might seem a bit trivial right now. You must see that an action needs to be connected to a purpose, a real purpose that reflects the 'self' that we are."

"It makes action actionable," said the Product Manager.

The heads around the table turned to the Product Manager, who was smiling at his own joke. "Seriously, it helps us go from something like, 'being the market leader,' which you, individually, can't seem to do much about because it's so general, to specific actions that are tied to motivation. I get it."

"Ok, Stan, I've suspended my disbelief for long enough in this conversation," said the Assistant Director, "Now for the real question. How does this help us connect with the marketplace and with our customers?"

"It helps us get into character, the character of the customer," Stanislavski responded. "And it describes what actions will connect the corporate 'self' to the customer."

"The character of the customer. Sounds like a great title for a book, Stan." The Research Manager was always trying to ingratiate himself, but Stanislavski made a mental note of it. One way or another, this story would make a wonderful addition to his autobiography.

"If we don't describe our actions correctly," the Assistant Manager interrupted, finishing Stanislavski's initial thought, "no one will be able to do what needs to be done."

"Yes, but it's more than that," Stanislavski said. "We also have to think about action as it applies to our customers. Don't forget, there are the actions of the customer to consider as well. Think for a second about a customer's actions when first confronted with a new pricing strategy. How might you describe a purchase in that situation?"

An uncomfortable silence ensued. Stanislavski let it persist. Finally the Communications Manager ventured a hesitant guess. "Something to do with expressing customer loyalty?" she offered.

"A good start, but not specific enough."

It was the Assistant Director who broke the silence this time. "Maybe it is something like, re-evaluating the value of our products? If they think the price is too high, they would be *attempting to preserve their self respect by declining to receive a disproportionate reward relative to the price paid for one of our products.* I think customers would decide to buy our products in spite of a pricing change if they think they will come out on the right side of the value equation. *Trying to beat the system*, how's that an acceptable action?"

He thought for a moment, as did the rest of the team. "That sounds reasonable," he replied. "We've just spent the whole morning sitting around talking about what action is," Stanislavski said. "Maybe it's time to take some action and *satisfy our hunger*. In other words, go get lunch. We can talk more about how to describe customer actions over a few sandwiches. Think of it as embarking on an excursion to replenish our creative spirits."

Without missing a beat (something we will learn more about later) the Research Manager added, "Now that's an action I can get motivated for."

Together they left the room, through the door this time, and headed down the street to the Product Manager's favorite deli.

* * * * * *

So what are you doing right now?

If your answer is that you are reading a book, that response would not have been enough for Stanislavski. By itself, reading is not an "action."

"Always act with a specific purpose in mind," Stanislavski said over and over in his writing. He did not believe in the "general" when it came to acting. In Stanislavski's world there were no general attributes, general feelings, general actions or, for that matter, *general reading of a book*. To help his actors express their actions in as specific a manner as possible, Stanislavski used question like: *Is the specific action capable of being completed? Is the action logical? Is it coherent? What is the motivation behind what you say you are doing? Does the action express the real truth of who you are?*

You must accept that every time a customer interacts with a company they are taking action. The action of the customer is not defined by the behavior but rather by the underlying motivation the customer is trying to satisfy. It is critical that companies understand the true actions of their customers as they act in the marketplace.

The job of the marketing professional is both to identify the actions taking place in the marketplace and to execute courses of action that match the resources and motivations of the company with the resources and motivations of the marketplace. Action, in the corporate world, is the coordinated movement of resources to meet a purpose, and the questions raised by Stanislavski are equally as relevant for each of the individual assets a company brings to bear in supporting its competitive position. Finding the right way to define corporate and customer actions according to the questions of Stanislavski's method offers clear direction for linking a company's capabilities to the motivations of the marketplace.

Let's take another look at action. According to Stanislavski an action is:

- Physically capable of being done

- Specific

- Not an errand

- Not presuppose any physical or emotional state

Remember, an activity is not an action and at any given time a single action can involve any one of many activities. Given that criterion, what action are you taking right now as you read this book? Let us suggest a couple of possibilities.

- Learning something that will help me to do my job better
- Acting on the recommendation of a friend or colleague (and deciding whether or not to trust that friend again in the future)
- Entertaining myself on a long (and boring) flight
- Deciding whether or not to change professions and become an actor

A true action is always tied to motivation. That's the reason most corporate strategies and "action plans" would fail any and all of Stanislavski's tests, as did the phrase, "to be the market leader" in the story we've just presented. The statement is not specific enough to be defined as an action, and does not contain enough information to be judged on the criteria outlined above. Likewise, most market research and observation fails to define customer actions in a way that marketers can effectively use to better align with their markets and facilitate exchanges.

Take a moment and look around you, inconspicuously of course, and observe the people around you. Try to look through their activities and see their actions. If you can spend a few minutes thinking about underlying actions of others, you'll begin to get the feel for what Stanislavski was trying to accomplish. Now let's turn the page, to satisfy our curiosity, and see how Stanislavski and his team use their lunch hour to put into practice the *theory* of action when observing customers in marketplace situations.

Scene IV

Observation

Because seeing is believing

It's true, that seeing is believing. But seeing, can also be understanding. In the next scene our characters find that by observing behavior the Stanislavski way, they can better understand the actions and motivations of customers as they act in the marketplace.

* * * *

"I know just the place for lunch," the Product Manager said as they all walked out of the room feeling energized by the morning's discussion of action.

Together the group went down in the elevator, through the lobby and out the front door of the building onto the busy street. Pointing the way, the Product Manager led the group to a deli. "One of my favorite places," he confessed to Stanislavski as they walked. "You'll love their Reuben."

"I don't suppose they are likely to have borsht there," he thought to himself, feeling a bit homesick. But his hopes soon changed when he saw the name of the deli: The St. Petersburger Deli.

"You should feel at home here," the Assistant Director commented. The group laughed, and with Stan in the lead they entered the store and walked toward the **Order Here** sign.

In front of the group was a line of customers, each waiting for their orders to be completed. A gentleman working behind the deli counter recognized the Product Manager and approached the group while calling out his name to get their attention.

"He's a pretty good guy, he owns this place," the Product Manager said to Stanislavski. "Russian parents, I think you'll like him."

Shaking the Product Manager's hand over the counter, the Deli Owner smiled and said, "You brought the whole group today? Are you expecting some sort of kickback?"

"Fifteen percent, that's all. So, what's good today?"

"You don't happen to have borsht, do you?" Stanislavski asked hopefully.

"Aren't you in luck! I made some fresh this morning. I think it's great, but a meat and potatoes guy like this," the Deli Owner said, pointing to the Product Manager, "he'd hate it."

"It had better be good," the Product Manager replied with a gravity that feigned true seriousness. "That's my boss. His name is Stan."

The Deli Owner reached over the counter and shook hands with Stanislavski. "Stan, good to meet you. I'll be right back with the best borscht you've had in a long while. And when I get back," he said to his friend, "I'll take your order for one of my gourmet *impress-the-boss* sandwiches. People are impressed by gourmet-sandwich-orderers." The Deli Owner smiled at the word he had contrived to fit the moment. "You wouldn't want to look cheap in front of the new boss, would you?"

The deli owner turned away to fill this next order. While they waited, Stanislavski turned to the group. "Did you notice, he used a joke to lead you to an action that was favorable to him?"

"That's normal," the Product Manager said. "As you've seen since you've gotten here, that's the kind of guy I am."

"And he knew that. He evaluated his resources and adapted his internal range to address yours." Stanislavski paused for a moment and slowed to emphasize the point. "He aligned his character to yours. To be able to do that, at one time or another, he had to *become* you, in a way. He had to figure out what you are like and find out how you respond to things, like to jokes for instance."

"He anticipated that your order, while an activity, was also an action and he figured he could influence your action because he observed that you are here with your new boss," replied Stanislavski. "He connected with you and surmised that you would want your action to be *to impress your boss*. Somewhere in his *self* he was able to retrieve that feeling and connect with it to understand how your character felt at this moment in the production that is the marketplace. Good for him."

"Do you think it was that calculated and deliberate," asked the Assistant Director of no one in particular.

"It might be conscious, it might not be," Stanislavski continued. "In fact, its best when it's not conscious, then it happens naturally. But to train ourselves to do that, or to train an organization or a company to do it, that's a different challenge. We're looking for tools that will help us do that. We're trying to understand ourselves so that we can determine which of our resources to call on to address situations head-on and make the best connections we can make. The first tool is learning how to observe. We need to go beyond simple observation and observe more deeply. We need to use our skills to observe details so we can identify and replicate actions. We need to systematically observe things, people, customers, everything and anything we encounter."

The Deli Owner returned with the bowl of borsht on a tray, with a spoon and napkin placed to the right of the bowl. "Almost as good as my grandmother's," he smiled. "Hope you like it." He then solicited orders from the rest of the team.

Stanislavski took the tray and noticed some empty tables at the back of the deli shop. He went over to the one farthest away from the counter, sat down, and waited for the rest of the team to join him. One by one, they sat down with their food. As they sat down they were instructed to keep an eye on the customers going in and out through the door. Stanislavski started the process of probing and questioning, not for specific answers, but to prod observational skills in his staff. He wanted to understand what they saw and how they saw it.

The first thing he asked of his company of budding thespians was for each one to recall, without looking, what the others had ordered, how they had ordered it and why they thought their colleague ordered what they ordered. He asked then to identify the action in each of their choices. The Communications Director was first. When identifying the salad choice made by the Assistant Director she hesitated, a bit nervous about the implications of suggesting the action was to maintain an attractive appearance. She didn't want to sound inappropriate or insulting. Emboldened by Stan's prompting she offered the explanation.

Recognizing the action in the hesitation, Stanislavski continued the conversation. "Actions cannot be tainted or influenced by concern for their impact on others," he said. "An action is an action independent of its," he paused for a moment trying to recall the term he had heard on the radio the day before, "Political correctness," he concluded.

Next he had them turn their attention to the front door as a professional looking woman walked confidently through the door talking on a cell phone while fumbling for her wallet in her purse.

"Where do you think she's just been?" Stanislavski asked the Research Manager.

"Work," the Research Manager said.

"Or shopping," the Communications Manager said.

"I'm pretty sure it's work," the Research Manager repeated.

"Why do you think that?" Stanislavski asked.

"Wearing sneakers with her business suit. That's a common dress code for professional women these days; sneakers out of the office, dress shoes in the office. Comfort, that's the action."

"That's not fair," the Assistant Director interrupted. "Look at what I've got on my feet, same shoes as in the office."

"You probably didn't have time to change," the Product Manager laughed. Realizing that he was right, she laughed with him before another person walked in through the front door.

"Nice suit," the Product Manager said.

"How much do you think it costs?" Stan asked.

"Probably somewhere in the $1,000 range. He's got to be a lawyer," the Product Manager responded.

Stanislavski turned to the Research Manager and posed the next question to him. "Why would a person buy a $1,000 suit?"

"You're asking the wrong person," the Research Manager said, loosening up for the first time since the gourmet meal incident. "You don't pay me enough and, with my kids just getting into high school…"

"He's asking you for a raise, Stan, be careful," the Product Manager interrupted as he gently poked Stanislavski in the arm.

"No, seriously," the Research Manager continued, "I'm not the kind of person who would buy a $1,000 suit, so it's kind of difficult for me to answer."

Stanislavski leaned forward and spoke a bit more slowly. "That's the point. You have to unlearn that limitation. What if we made $1,000 suits? What would you do? How would you put yourself in the mind of someone who would buy a $1,000 suit? This is exactly what we've been talking about."

"Don't get me wrong, I'd love to be able to buy a $1,000 suit, it's not that hard to imagine."

"Why?" asked Stanislavski. "Do you buy the suit because you have the money or do you buy it because you want to look like you have the money? Do $1,000 suits really feel better than $300 suits when you wear them?"

"Yeah, that's an interesting question," the Product Manager added, challenging the Research Manager a bit. "Does he or doesn't he?"

"What?"

"Have the money?"

The Research Manager looked closely at the man as he ordered his sandwich, and walked around the store looking at the various items on the shelves. After a minute, he said with some authority, "No. He doesn't have the money."

"Doesn't?" the Communications Manager said. "Looks like it to me."

"Sure you don't want to ask him out for a date," the Product Manager whispered to her. The question made her blush. Stanislavski noticed it and made a mental note of her reaction.

"No," the Research Manager began a bit slowly, "no, it's the shoes. They're worth about fifty or sixty bucks, maximum. Anyone knows that you invest in your feet if you've got the money but it's also the part of

71

your attire you think you can hide; you know, behind the desk, under the table. I think that he doesn't have the money for the expensive suit and the expensive shoes, so he chose the suit to give the impression that he had money. Comfort wasn't his motivation, image was."

The Communications Manager was not convinced, which lead the Product Manager to call over his friend, the Deli Owner, when the man with the $1,000 dollar suit left the store.

"Do you know that guy?" asked the Product Manager.

"Sure do," responded the Deli Owner. "Comes here pretty often. He's a paralegal, really wants to be a lawyer, wants to stand up with the big shots in his firm, but can't do it. My guess is he doesn't have the money for law school. He's just turned thirty and has a young kid. He's always talking about the 'big mortgage' and the 'big debts'. Says he can't ever just get ahead. It's actually kind of sad. He's a real nice guy."

"Do you mind if I ask you something?" Stanislavski interrupted

"Sure. Anyone who eats my borsht as enthusiastically as you did can ask me anything you want."

"What did he order for lunch?"

The Deli Owner smiled, getting the connection immediately. "The St. Pertersburger. Get it? It's actually a small hamburger with one slice of American cheese on a Kaiser roll but it sounds fancier that way. Lots of people get it. It's inexpensive, but filling.

"I didn't even notice that," the Research Manager said.

"Which is just as important," said Stanislavski. "Observing character, in preparation for becoming a character, requires a number of different perspectives. Collect as many perspectives as you can about your customers, from as many sources as you can find. Then, add them up and sketch out a complete picture of a character. Now that's a challenge."

Stanislavski then turned to the Assistant Director. "Now, if our observations are correct, describe the action of that man buying a $1,000 suit."

The Assistant Director put her fork down and thought about it for a moment. Finally she said, "Buying a suit to impress my co-workers."

"Close," Stanislavski responded, "but not quite. That presupposes an emotional state on the part of the co-workers. They'd have to be impressed with a $1,000 suit."

"I'd be impressed with a $1,000 suit," the Product Manager said.

"We've established that much," the Assistant Director said, covering up her slight embarrassment in not getting it right the first time. "How about, buying a suit *to bolster my self-esteem*?"

"Better, much better. You've connected a sense of self, to an observation, to an action with a motivation that meets the criterion we spoke about. And, it gets at the heart of purchasing behavior for that person."

Just as Stanislavski explained this final bit of characterization, the CEO walked in. The Deli Owner moved to greet him and asked what he wanted. Waving to Stanislavski and the marketing team, he asked for a Reuben sandwich.

He then looked at the potato chip rack just below the deli counter. He thought for a second, smiled, and picked out a bag of sour cream and onion chips before walking over to the table. The momentary change in facial expression did not go unnoticed by Stanislavski. "Mind if I join you," asked the CEO. "I really needed to get out of the office." Noticing the open note pads scattered around the table he asked. "Are you on some sort of field trip?"

"In a manner of speaking," answered Stanislavski. "I guess you could call it a field trip, although this is not really a field."

"It's St. Petersburg," joked the Product Manager. "We brought Stan home."

"Please, have a seat," the Assistant Director said, gesturing to a free chair close to the table.

As the CEO sat down, Stanislavski asked him "So we've identified from your comment that your action is to get away from work for a bit. Now, why did you choose that bag of potato chips?"

"They're good and they're my one weakness in the ongoing struggle with my waistline," he laughed.

"You smiled when you picked up the bag of chips. Why this kind of chips over another? What was the action of your behavior?"

"I can't say, really, partly because I'm not entirely sure what you're asking. I chose these chips, I guess, because I was in the mood for a pick me up," he replied.

Validated that the smile he had observed was in fact meaningful, he asked, "Any specific memories about sour cream and onion potato chips?"

"Stan, I didn't know you were a psychologist," interjected the Product Manager.

"Marketing, psychology, acting," the CEO casually commented. "All the same in the end, right Stan?" He quickly moved the conversation back to Stanislavski's question, saying, "I've got a lot of memories about sour cream and onion potato chips and corporate lunches. But it really started with my father and my sister, who loved these things. There was always a bag around the house since my father would buy them whenever they were on sale. My mother would hide them, hoping that my sister and I wouldn't eat them but we would always find them and then we would go out back together and polish off a bag behind the big tree in the backyard."

"So," the Communications Manager commented, "it all began with your sister."

"Yeah. She and her husband and their kids live overseas and we don't see each other much these days. When I eat them I think of her. These days, I guess I use them as an excuse for getting out of the office. I was thinking earlier today that it will be her birthday next week so I guess I was just trying to go *out back* and polish off a bag with her."

"And look, we're all out there with you," added the Research Manager in a sympathetic gesture.

They all laughed somewhat awkwardly as the deli owner brought over the sandwich.

"So," the Deli Owner asked Stanislavski, "you liked the borsht, yes?"

"Almost as good as my mother's," he smiled. "She used to make borsht every week back in Moscow. Boy was it good."

"I knew it, I knew it as soon as you walked through the door," the Deli Owner said, a bit excited.

"Oh, how could you tell?" Stanislavski asked putting on an air of surprise, but the CEO, as always, seemed to raise his guard against potential difficulties in the official Stan Islavski storyline.

"Only a Russian would jump as quickly as you did at the chance of eating borsht. Govorite po-russki?"

"What was that?" asked the CEO.

"He asked me if I spoke Russian. Da. Ya gavaruyu po-russki. Eta moye rodnoi yazyk."

"Very nice, music to my ears," said the Deli Owner. "So where were you born, Stan? Your accent sounds ... old Muscovite."

"Well," the CEO cut in, trying to end the conversation. "I've got to get back to the office."

"I guess this proves your point again, Stan, that the method works," said the Assistant Director. Stan and the CEO traded suspicious glances.

"Method? My method certainly works," the Deli Owner said with some pride in his voice. "My method for making borsht is best in the area."

"No, we were really talking about your method for approaching your business and your customers," the Assistant Director said. "We're on an observation mission. We're observing the marketplace and identifying action in our subjects. I've been observing you. You're somewhat complicated but at the same time very simple. You connect with people through humor. You use humor and compassion and sometimes understanding to soften the sale and make people forget they are spending their hard earned money with you. You are very good at catering to the character of your customers."

"It's a bit more than just picking out the characteristics of the customer, though," Stanislavski jumped in. "You see, you have to put yourselves in the mind of the customer. From conception … from a thought like, 'I will make borsht today and offer it as the special!' … to an action tied to a motivation, like, 'making borscht *to offer an item of which I am proud.*'"

"From there," Stanislavski continued, "we move to the internal resources of the 'self' and the 'self' asks, what experiences have I had with borsht? What do I remember about those experiences? What do I really know about making borsht? What have I observed from people who have made borsht? What have I observed about myself making borsht?" Stanislavski took a long theatrical pause.

"I've always wondered what's in borsht," quipped the Research Manager.

Stanislavski ignored the question and continued. "The next step in the method is to put yourself in the mind of the customer and ask yourself how you would act if you were the customer. What kind of action and motivation would be behind a borsht purchase?" He scanned the table for reactions. No one seemed to have a clue.

"There's more," he continued, "but you're not ready yet. We have much to do and little time. I'm don't want to get ahead of myself. If I keep going, I'll have nothing left to share with you over the course of the next several weeks."

"Weeks?" the CEO said, covering the mistake Stanislavski had just made. "Stan, I expect that with that kind of thinking, you'll be sharing your insights with us for a long time."

"Of course," said Stanislavski regaining his composure and getting himself quickly back into character. "A very long time, sir."

The CEO paid the bill and everyone returned to the office. During the course of the walk back there was minimal conversation but there was a great deal of observation related commentary.

* * * * * *

Observation is an actor's form of market research. It is one of the ways an actor gathers information, adding to the inventory of knowledge maintained by the self. The collection of observations is a process of developing an inventory from which to draw for a role.

The skill of observation is also critically important in successful marketing. Observation goes beyond simply seeing an action. It is the act of seeing an action in the context of a situation and individual. This skill is essential at all levels of the marketing process. Traditional marketing observation focuses on quantifying fixed parameters. It approaches observation as the identification of demographics and trends. What we can learn from Stanislavski's Method is the application of observation to the identification of the actions associated with consumer behavior. With that we can align the range of our corporate self to those actions and present an appropriate self to the markets.

Our players did a little bit of 'people watching' in the last scene, and got a better understanding of the details an actor looks for in stretching the scope of one's observations. It's worth doing a bit of the same the next time you are in an environment where people are buying things, asking questions like:

- What are the actions (not behavior) that you are observing?

- How do customers interact with a particular product? Do they want to reach out and touch it or is seeing it enough?

- What are the customers wearing? Is there any informative consistency in appearance for the customers of a particular product or service that's not apparel?

- Why do you think a customer is motivated to make a choice of one product over another? What are some of the actions that a customer would take to reveal that motivation?

- Where was the customer before purchasing a particular product? Is their sequencing of events relevant in their purchase decision?

- What in the element or range of elements within your corporate self best prepares you to connect with that customer? How can you adapt the elements of your corporate self to connect with what you have just observed?

This will give you a general sense of how to describe customers acting in the marketplace. Now think abstractly about your customers or the customers of a specific company. That's the theme of the next, more magical chapter.

Scene V

The Magic *If*

If I were king of the forest ...

That was the "if" imagined by the Cowardly Lion in <u>*The Wizard of Oz*</u> as he described all the things he would do. In this scene, our players discover that the imagination embodied in *if* can lead to action in the forest they know as the competitive marketplace.

* * * *

Several days later, back at the office, Stanislavski gathered his thoughts alone in his office before starting the next session with his staff. It was fortunate that the CEO recognized the problem he would have paying the bill back at the deli as payroll had been having problems processing the identification information he had given them, asking repeatedly for something called a social security number or green card. As a result, his first paycheck had yet to arrive, weeks after starting his assignment.

"Practicing the power of observation," the CEO had said to him as they peeled off from the larger group on the way back to the office from the deli several days earlier. "That's not a bad way to start them out on building a character, but you're going to have to go deeper than that; it makes for interesting conversation, but if it doesn't increase revenues its just an exercise."

Stanislavski continued the thought. "Absolutely. Nothing happens until an actor stretches beyond observation and learns how to internalize the character."

"Have you started on the internalization process?"

"Not yet."

"You better move fast," the CEO said. "You don't have much time left."

It looked like Stanislavski would have to perform some magic. Fortunately, he had taken some lessons from one of his past plays. He thought about the conversation for the better part of a week while his staff processed the information they had collected and completed a few more sessions on basic observational skills.

When the time came to press farther into the external challenge he and the CEO had mapped out, he walked into the conference room, greeted his staff, turned to the whiteboard in front of him and wrote one word: "**IF**"

"This," he said, "this is our magic. One word. *If.*"

They had all begun to expect the unexpected from Stan, but none of them understood where he was going with this one.

"*The magic if.* It's the basis of our profession. Take a lesson from Shakespeare: *If* I was Othello, and Iago had told me of Desdimona's infidelity, *I would feel jealous.* How about ones from our recent excursion: *If* I was a CEO feeling lonely for family abroad, *I would choose sour cream potato chips.* How about: *If* I was Stan Islavski in a Russian deli, *I would choose a home cooked meal, the borsht, over all other choices.*"

"The equations sound easy enough, but to successfully connect with customers and markets you need the right equations, the ones that work for connecting both your *self* and this company's character with that of the customer. And doing that involves more than simply observing a customer." He paused unnecessarily for effect. "They say that a great character actor must internalize his character and understand, in a fundamental way, the character's motivation if he wants to become the character. I say that's what we, as great marketers, need to do with our customers."

As Stanislavski paused to catch his breath, the Assistant Director chimed in, "And if we go back to some of the discussions we've had over the past few weeks, the character..." she chuckled as she caught herself, "I mean the customer, the customer doesn't just exist when a sale is made and they take action. Customers exist before and after an action is taken and, when you observe the before and after, you learn how to describe the motivation."

"That's right," Stanislavski continued, "No single event occurs in isolation. They all come from a whole, the whole being the character of the customer. *Why a cheap burger at a fancy deli?* Because a flashy suit makes him feel important. I bet he wouldn't eat the cheap burger if he wasn't alone. *Why cheap shoes?* Because the kids need braces and family comes first. You see, you cannot understand the motivations of the paralegal as your customer until you have put yourself in his shoes."

Then the Research Manager, with an expectant voice, asked, "So how do we get into the shoes of our customer?"

"Let's hope our customer's shoes smell better than mine do," the Product Manager joked.

"I'll give you an example," Stanislavski said as he developed a cover story in his mind for the material he was about to present. "It's a story related to me by a good friend whose brother's wife's cousin was an actress. At a rehearsal during her first days in drama school, she was given a scenario to act out as follows: *You are to play a woman whose mother has just lost her job and income. You now have no money left to pay for your school tuition. But a friend has come to your rescue by offering to give a fine brooch with precious stones, valuable enough to meet the rest of your needs for the remainder of the school term. You are unsure whether you should accept it, so the friend sticks the brooch into a curtain before you are able to refuse. You chase the friend out of the room, and try to convince the friend to take the brooch back. Eventually you are convinced to accept the gift. If you returned to the room and could not find the brooch, what would you do?* The scene began there, with that *if.*"

Stanislavski paused for a moment to make sure his team understood the scenario for the character.

"The first time through the exercise, my friend's brother's wife's cousin quickly dashed onto the stage, ran her hands through the curtains, put on an expression of disbelief, and did all of the things that a below average actor does to represent looking for a brooch. Upon leaving the stage, the Director stopped her and asked, "Where's the brooch?" She stopped and said, "I didn't find one." The Director responded, "There is a brooch in the curtain. I put one there before the beginning of the exercise, and, if you can not find it, I will not permit you to continue in this class." The woman immediately rushed back to the curtain and did what anyone in the situation would do; she began a painstaking search through the curtain to find the brooch, which, of course, wasn't really there."

"What the director taught her," Stanislavski concluded, "was that the magic if only works when you internalize the character in a specific way. The director created an analogous situation and the actor was required to live those moments in a way that helped her understand the character in that moment as a part of her *self*."

Stanislavski feared, based on the expressions around the room, that he had gotten off track and his mind was racing to try to connect this story back to the task at hand. The Assistant Director stepped in to *breach the broach divide*, as she put it, and made the connection. "It's more than understanding the customer, or focusing on the customer, it's actually recognizing the things we have in common with the customer, the parts of the customer that are parts of our *selves*, and building from those insights."

"Exactly," Stanislavski said, "that's exactly it. We have to connect our self to the self of the customer. And because our self is a collection of the experiences it has collected and the resources it has developed, we should ask what we have in common with our customers. Let's start there."

The team reflected on this for a moment before the Product Manager interrupted the silence. "Here's something that I have in common with some of our customers," he said. "Some of our product lines are targeted to children, but, as everyone knows, to sell to children you also have to sell to parents, because the parents are the ones who have the money. I've got children, and I get pulled by the kids into buying things I don't think we need."

"What is the relationship between you and your kids like, on purchasing issues," the Research Manager probed.

"I try to buy things that are good for them, they try to buy things that are bad for them. I look for simple, safe toys. They look for complicated toys with lots of parts. Contentious but conciliatory, that's the relationship." Members of the team laughed and the Product Manager continued. "Seriously, we look at products differently. I guess we value them differently."

"If you were in a store, then," Stanislavski probed, "and I asked you to talk about a range of things you would find in the store, the values you would look for would be..."

"Safety of the products, reliability, quality and above all, ease of assembly. You know, all the good stuff. I'd say they are more interested in fun." The Product manager struggled with the *if* proposition a bit more before coming out with one emphatic statement: "I want to be able to look at a product and feel that the company has demonstrated to me a knowledge of what's good for both me and my kids."

"That's really interesting," the Assistant Director said. "I don't have any children yet, but hearing it from your perspective, I can see how that would be really important to a parent. I have two dogs and I am very protective of them. Maybe that's a part of my self I can draw on in this particular situation."

Stanislavski saw a dynamic developing that was similar to those he experienced in some of the best acting groups in the world; an ability to pool experiences and insights to understand a plot, a character or a play. "This is just the sort of thinking we need to do more of," he commented. "Eventually, if we probe through our products and question our own personal experiences, we will go one step farther than observation. This company, taken as a whole, is probably representative of almost any customer group we would want to work with. The motivation of every individual customer is likely here in our 'self' someplace. We must draw from our corporate and individual selves to find them. Don't worry, I promise we will do more of that type of exercise during this phase of our planning."

"How about we go one step farther," offered the Research Manager. "Let's actually ask the same question of a customer."

"Alright," replied Stanislavski. "But this time, let's ask one of *our* customers."

"I know just the guy," the Product Manager said as he pulled over the phone that had been sitting in the middle of the conference room table. He hit the button for speakerphone and, before anyone could ask him who he was calling, he punched in a number and the phone began to ring.

"You'll love this guy," he said to Stanislavski. "He's about a crazy as they come."

"Who is he?" Stanislavski asked.

"He's a reseller, owns a chain of retail stores in zone two," the Product Manager explained. "He purchases some of our products directly, and he also uses some of our distribution partners. It also helps that he's a personal friend from college."

"Yello!" The voice on the other end played with the vowels and stretched the word out for a few seconds before the Product Manager cut him off.

"Hey, it's me."

"Me? Me? I don't know anyone named me." It was clear that the man knew exactly who it was. "You must have the wrong number."

"It's always the wrong number when I call you." The Product Manager turned serious for a moment. "Listen, I've got my boss here on the speakerphone."

"Oh, no wonder you called on my private line," the friend interrupted. "So, I guess that means I have to switch to my respectable voice and demeanor."

"That won't be necessary," Stanislavski said, leaning up to the phone and speaking very loudly. He had seen the CEO use one of these speaker phone things before, but it was a new experience for him. He spoke slowly, as if stretching his voice over a long distance. "It takes all sorts of characters to make a world."

"Always a kidder," the Product Manager said, a bit nervous that his friend might take the comment as an insult. "How about we get down to business?"

"Here's what we're doing," the Assistant Director began. "We're doing a bit of informal research on the general interests and motivations of our customers. Trying to assess what they think is valuable about products and services. Basically, we want to know what your customers think is valuable about our products and our company."

"And I figured you were a cheap and easy audience for us." The Product Manager turned and winked at Stanislavski clearly proud of his extension of Stan's incessant acting references. Then he turned back to the phone and added, "I could make it up to you the next time we're out on the golf course by giving you a couple of strokes..."

"How about offering something I need!" the customer interrupted. "Seriously, all of you do that, and it always gets on my nerves."

"What, what did I do," the Product Manager responded, a bit concerned that this comment ran deeper than the common jokes they shared.

"You just did it again," the Customer said. "You're always asking about what *my* customers want. That's fine, that's important, but *I'm* one of *your* customers too. Ask about me! And tell me, what are you guys doing with your pricing? Are you trying to put me out of business?"

"You've got me," the Product Manager commented. "I told you what I thought last time we got together."

Stanislavski cut in. "I'm new here. To be honest, I'd rather talk to you and just get to know *you*. Then I can get to know you as a customer. And, if we have time, maybe then we can talk about your customers."

"Now that sounds like a change of pace," the voice from the box responded. "Shoot. Ask me anything you'd like."

Stanislavski thought for a moment about where to begin, and then decided to go with the unconventional but familiar question. "If I was playing you in a Broadway show or a Hollywood film, what would you want me to know about you in preparation for the part?"

"Wow, what kind of a question is that?"

"The guy is obsessed with the theater and the classics," the Product Manager replied. "But, humor him, he is my boss, and I can make it worth your time."

"Hey, I've got no problem with the question. I've always thought they should make a full length feature of my life. I'm thinking one of those big muscular action-hero types as me, with the scrawny nerdy type playing my good friend there." He was obviously referring to the Product Manager.

"Your life is like an action movie, is that what you're trying to tell us?" asked the Assistant Director.

"Absolutely," the customer responded, playing along with the Assistant's joke. "Something always going on around here. You've got to stay flexible 'cause there's a lot of demands, so I guess I'd be looking for an actor that could do all sorts of things."

The Research Manager leaned forward to pose the next question. "What's your workday like?"

"I'm an early riser, usually into the office by about six-thirty or seven in the morning. I try to get out in time to eat dinner with the family around six or seven at night. I'll do some more work from home in the evenings and on the weekends, so I guess you can say that my workday doesn't really stop."

Stanislavski asked the next question. "Do you enjoy it?"

"Enjoy it? Enjoy it?" Stanislavski noticed a distinct change in the Customer's tone. "This isn't the kind of job you enjoy. It's nothing but problems and troubleshooting."

The Assistant Director took up the line of questioning. "What do you hate most about your work?"

"I want to be able to make decisions quickly and move on. The problem is that there are some decisions I can make, others I can't. Buying from you is a great example. I sign a contract with you, you supply us, and you think it's all over. The purchase is not really a one time thing, you see," the customer responded. "Because I have multiple stores, each one with its own demo, I have special needs when it comes to configurations, quantities, returns, delivery, you know, everything."

"He's worth a lot of revenue to us," whispered the Product Manager to Stanislavski.

"It's a relationship issue, rather than a point of sale issue," the voice continued from the telephone. "There are a number of connections which a company like yours has to make at levels above and below me — distributors, smaller chains, and single point outlets — and that's where you're weak. I can talk to you all you want about your products, but I'm pretty much convinced that your stuff is good."

"...and my kickbacks don't hurt, do they?" added the Product Manager.

"No, they don't, but if you don't start paying attention to the other people, the decision makers who don't interface directly with you during a purchase decision, you're going to lose market share. There are a number of different scenarios out here in the market. The general impression of the market is that you just don't understand. You have your opinions and that's that. You have to understand that there are things that my customers need, things that I need as a customer and even things that my competitors need. You don't seem to have that kind of range." Everyone in the room looked up at Stanislavski as they all caught his unintended reference. "It's as if, and I don't mean to offend anyone, if you haven't done it, you can't apply yourself to do it."

A quick scan of the room showed Stanislavski that the disclaimer hadn't worked. There were definitely some wounded feelings in the group. Stanislavski just smiled.

"Alright, let me ask you this," the Assistant Director chimed in. "What are the other companies providing competing products saying and doing that we're not?"

She looked over at Stanislavski, who appeared to have a different question in his eyes. She took a step back from this specific question and went to one that sounded more like an actress sizing up the environment in which her character would operate.

"Strike that. How about this question: How would you characterize your interaction with these people, your customers, suppliers and employees? What sorts of things do you talk about, what are the issues of concern to them? What motivates each of you?"

Stanislavski scanned the room as the team listened to the response. "Well, it depends on who you are talking about. With my suppliers, it's often a bit contentious. We haggle and jockey for position. We each want the upper hand. I have to protect myself by knowing the ramifications of every negotiation and every interaction. Often times it's not price, but rather the extras. When will I get it, what payment terms, are there any funds available for promotion?"

"And what about your customers?" asked the Research Manager.

"My customers want to know that they are getting their money's worth. They want to know that the products I am selling them will meet their needs, will not break, will be safe, and will be a good value for the money. They also want the experience of purchasing the item to be a pleasant one. They come to me because they want something. Sometimes I can help and sometimes I can't. What frustrates us both is not that I can't help them, but rather that I can't help them."

"You been drinking?" the Product Manager asked, joking with his old friend. "You're repeating yourself, again."

"No, I meant what I said. What frustrates me is when I want to help them and I can't. If it's a matter of the customer wanting the product for less than is reasonable or wanting a delivery that is impossible and we can't reach a compromise, then I can't help and that's alright. But when they have a need and I know that I should be able to help but can't, that's frustrating. If my price from you is too high, I can't make the sale. If you don't make the product in the right configuration, I can't make the sale. And if you don't stand behind the integrity of your products, then I am definitely outta luck." He paused for a moment, "Sorry, I guess I got up on my soap box for a minute. I don't mean to beat you guys up with my frustrations. It's just my intention to make a sale and have a happy customer. That starts with how we interact. Relatively speaking, you guys are good at working with me."

"I'm glad to hear that," the Assistant Director asked, "I was getting a bit nervous."

"Now you know how I feel," the voice continued, "afraid you might lose a customer. It's scary to think that a customer is dissatisfied and may go elsewhere."

Stanislavski let that comment sink in. This customer had been a real help and he had given Stanislavski an opportunity to return to the *Magic If*.

"If I was you, and I felt that I wasn't being supported, what would I do?" he asked the Customer. "If I couldn't help a customer, how would I feel?" The questions were posed to the Customer but clearly intended for the marketing team.

"And if I were you, my old friend," the man on the phone added, clearly talking to his old friend, "I'd get my, uh, butt down here and take me out to lunch and make things right again."

"Listen, we've taken up a great deal of your time," Stanislavski commented sensing that it was time to conclude the call and return to their work. "We appreciate the opportunity to speak with you about these issues. I'm going to be asking my staff to talk to all sorts of customers in the coming weeks and to ask all kinds of 'what if' questions. What we want to do is understand more than just what our customers want; we want to know what motivates our customers, what they are thinking, what their concerns are and how they would act in certain circumstances."

"Hey, it was good talking to me."

The Product Manager's joke brought the conversation to a conclusion. After the team expressed their thanks, the meeting turned to a diagnosis of the discussion's content. The team talked at length about some of the tactical issues they faced such as supply capacity, product lines, pricing, advertising, and distribution. The more the conversation continued the more Stanislavski allowed himself to sit back and observe the scene as it played out. After some time he started to feel that the conversation was becoming too granular, so he interjected in an effort to refocus the group on the overriding issue he was charged with fixing.

"Before an actor can act, he or she needs to know how, and why, to act." The group was becoming so accustomed to the analogies that the comment had no undermining effect on the "Stan" cover story. "That's true for this company as well," he continued. "In this discussion we've learned how this individual customer is motivated, how he acts, and that he would like us to act on his behalf."

The Assistant Director took the point one step further. "We learned about the people in the deli through observation. I guess the first step is observing actual customers and putting our skills to use."

"But it's more than just our customers, it's our competitors and their customers as well," the Product Manager added. "It's just as important to understand how the other players in our production act and to find out why people choose not to be our customers. While we're at it, we should observe people who aren't anyone's customer to find out what they're like and why they aren't consuming some form of our products. "

Stanislavski was pleased with the progress he was clearly making and thought back on the times when he had sent actors out to engage in observation for building a character. He realized that the logical next step for his students was to send them out on their own to observe. He didn't have a clue what he would do with the results, but he figured the least he could do was to provide one last direction.

"It is the *ifs* that matter. The *if* is our magic. Don't think about isolated characteristics, think about scenarios like where products are offered, when customers buy products, how they buy products, where they buy products and, most importantly, why they buy them. Collect your descriptions of their motivations, and always try to ask yourself the tough if questions about the person's behavior. Always wonder, *if I were this person or this company, how would I react?* Ask yourself, *if I were this customer or a competitor, why would I be doing what the customer or competitor is doing?* And remember, always search for the action which is hidden in the observation."

After a brief planning session the team divided up territories and markets, and decided to take the next two weeks to go out into the field and talk with anyone and everyone they could find within the key markets of the company. They code named it *Operation Observation* at the urging of the Research Manager. Being marketing people, they couldn't help but have shirts and hats made with the name of the new special operation embroidered on them. The next day, after the group left for the field, Stanislavski wore his shirt to the office with pride.

* * * * * *

Every great actor can perform a bit of magic just by using one simple word: *If.* Stanislavski would say that *if acts as a lever to lift us out of the world of actuality into the realm of imagination. As a tool for character development actors use "as if" propositions to better connect internal capabilities to specific actions and motivations.*

Marketing professionals need to use the same words every day, asking the question: *What if I was the customer?* The point that Stanislavski makes, though, is that the question should not be asked in isolation. The *if* performs no magic if it is merely an abstraction. *If* has to be personal, meaning that it must directly relate to the individual actions and motivations of the person asking the question.

Answering the question isn't as straightforward as you might think. For instance, "I would want good service if I were a customer" does not go far enough for Stanislavski because the phrase doesn't meet his criterion for how to describe actions and motivations. One clearly missing element is a motivation.

Here's a scenario for you to consider:

A customer wants to purchase a video camera. She's not interested in being sold by a salesperson but wants to buy the camera in person. She spends time looking through a camera book or looking around on the Internet for information. She finds one that she thinks would suit her, and, the next day, walks into a camera store close to where she works during her lunchtime break and casually walks up to the counter.

Your question is, *if you were the customer, what is the first question you would ask?*

Maybe it's about the availability of the specific model she has in mind. That would sound something like: *I'm interested in such and such a model. Do you have it in stock?*

What would motivate her to begin with that question? Let's say she needs to get back to the office quickly and doesn't have time to comparison shop. In that case, she asks specifically for the camera *to speed her purchase of the item.* Subsequent actions follow from that initial motivation, and you can see how the interaction between the woman and the sales person would proceed. The exchange would be based on quickly confirming the availability and quality of the product, the price and a quick decision would be made to buy or not to buy.

But what if, deep down, she wasn't secure in her decision? What would her approach be then? What would the clues that the salesperson could observe to distinguish one action from the other? What if the customer had opened with: *I want to buy such and such a camera – is that a good choice for me?* How can you be prepared, as either the company or the salesperson, to address the motivation that manifests itself in her action?

Ask yourself a series of questions: When have I been in this situation? What motivates me to walk into a certain store? How would I react if I heard that the model of the product I was looking for was not available? What if the salesperson told me that he didn't think the model was a good choice? What circumstances preceding the moment of sale would make me a committed product-specific shopper and what would leave me willing to hear other options? How can you discern the difference by observing the actions around you?

The point of this exercise is simple. If you understand and define the initial motivation correctly for a specific customer or market, you can sketch out a scenario leading to a successful conclusion which involves an exchange between any company and any customer. Over time you will build up a list of actions and motivations relating to your customers, ones that you might not have thought of before.

The next question is: What do you do with your newly minted list of motivations and actions? How do you put them to work? As you would expect, it's different in different situations. The key, as the next chapter points out, is learning where, when and how circumstances require the application of which specific internal capabilities and competencies of a company or individual wishing to effect a transaction in the marketplace.

Scene VI

The Unbroken Line

"All the king's horses and all the king's men,
couldn't put Humpty together again."

The famous nursery rhyme reminds us that putting it all together, or back together as the case may be, can be a difficult thing. This is true, even for an actor and director as accomplished as Stanislavski.

* * * * * * * *

It had been almost two months since Stanislavski's initial meeting with the marketing team of The Ater Company. As with many of the plays he had directed, time seemed to be passing at an unusually accelerated pace. The lessons had gone well so far and his staff was beginning to understand the fundamentals of the acting process. He felt that he had made a good connection between his skills and the marketing needs of the company by using terms like action, motivation, work on one's *self*, and the *magic if*. In response, his staff had conducted extensive interviews with people both inside and outside the company to identify the corporate *self*, understand its capabilities, and better define what he was now regularly referring to as *the character of the customer*.

"So Constantin, you've taught them about the internal and external challenges," the CEO had commented in a meeting to review Stanislavski's progress. "But I don't see the synthesis yet."

A bit more than half of the time allotted to him by the CEO had passed, and Stanislavski was beginning to feel increasing pressure to break through the initial preparatory work and reach the heart of the matter: connecting the company's capabilities, people and resources directly with the customers' needs. The unanswered question of how would he pull it all together in this context at this critical juncture of the process was beginning to concern him.

"My method has worked for me so far," Stanislavski said to himself after the review meeting with the CEO. "I guess I'll teach them exactly what I would start teaching actors at this point, how to pull it all together using the concept of the *Unbroken Line*."

The team assembled in the conference room where they first met, the Assistant Director, the Product Manager, Communications and Research Managers, and Constantin Stanislavski, a.k.a. Stan. Stanislavski looked somewhat more comfortable this time. Having bought a newly tailored black suit and shirt in the style of the CEO (and with the help of the CEO's personal assistant who he had jokingly referred to as the costume manager), he now looked more the part.

The other roles in the production had changed little in the interim. As usual, the Research Manager had prepared a set of slides, demonstrating in full-color the results of their work. This time, however, the people in the meeting allowed him to actually present some of what he had prepared.

The first part of the presentation consisted mostly of qualitative statements from interviews conducted with The Ater Company's employees about the corporate *self*. He followed the opening slides with ones that presented a sweeping review of customer observations and a summary of interviews about behaviors, actions and motivations connected to the character of the customer. To their credit, noted Stanislavski, they had expanded their research beyond simply purchasing circumstances. The presentation touched on the breadth of issues raised in the first interview conducted by the team, with elements of both work and home life integrated into the material. When he reached the point in the presentation where some synthesis was required, he stopped.

"You know," he said, turning on the lights in the room, "I drafted material to talk about the implications of all of this, but, to be honest, I think they're pretty mediocre."

The Research Manager's face registered disappointment, but Stanislavski sensed the time was right to pull together the material in a very different way than the Research Manager would have. Before revealing his synthesis, he turned to the Assistant Director to see how she pulled it together. "What do you think?" Stanislavski asked her.

"I think there are some solid themes coming from these results," the Assistant Director commented. "On the corporate *self* front, our people tended to characterize our strengths by pointing to what our products offer to our customers."

"But there are a lot of differences in statements of motivation and purpose of action," the Research Manager pointed out.

"If you ask me, that all ties back to who we are as a company," the Product Manager added.

Stanislavski leaned forward, and in a deliberately challenging voice asked the Product Manager to elaborate.

"Well, it has to do with our identity. After all, that's the core of our *self*. The answers to the questions of who we are as a company, what our collective corporate experience is, what our corporate range is, what it is we do here and what we really provide our customers were frankly all over the place. Each answer seemed to be a reflection of the individual answering. The answers reflected his or her strengths and his or her history of contributions to the company. It's like we have an individual and collective identity problem."

"Add in the answers from the customers," the Research Manager chimed in, "and you see that there's no consistent view at all of who we are, what our range is, what we do and what we provide. There was also no consensus on what we can do that we're not doing. There are a lot of individual pieces, all very relevant and very valuable, but also very diverse."

There was silence around the room as everyone present contemplated what to say next.

"This is something we've discussed before," the Assistant Director said breaking the silence. "We in marketing have an idea of what we do here and what motivates us. But it appears that those who are doing what it is we actually do here seem to have a different view of it."

Stanislavski quickly looked around the room, concluding it was time to press forward. "It seems that while we, this company, are doing something together as a corporate *self*, the individual actions need to be brought together in a more systematic way."

"Wait a minute," the Research Director objected. "What does that have to do with the functional breakout of the data I was describing?"

Stanislavski slapped his hand down on the table, stood, and walked slowly in the direction of the Research Manager. He leaned in and asked, "Do you think this discussion is a waste of time?"

Put back by Stan's abrupt action, the Research Manager could only respond, "Uh, no."

Stanislavski smiled, patted him on the back, and laughed. "I was just making a point. What do you think my intention was just now?"

"I guess it was to challenge me."

"Be more specific, phrase it in terms of an action ... what could I have been trying to do."

"How about: *letting me know who the boss is*."

"Ok, let's go with that one. My intention was to let you know who the boss is, to assert my position as *the boss*. That was my action. So what did I do to communicate that action?"

The Research Manager, finally realizing that this was just Stan making a point and not Stan actually being mad at him, calmed a bit and offered, "You asked me a question that asserted your position."

"And you shook your head from side to side as you let out a short sigh before getting up," added the Communications Manager.

"You also walked over and said it directly in his face," added the Product Manager.

"And you slammed your hands down before standing," added the Assistant Director. They were all clearly proud of what they considered to be their new found mastery of observation skills.

"That's correct," responded Stanislavski turning to her, "all of those were part of communicating my intention. That's a beat, the distance from the beginning of an intention to the end of an intention."

"It sure seemed that you wanted to beat me," joked the Research Manager.

"Every intention has a beginning and an end. The distance that an individual must travel varies based on the intention. Some intentions require a single line of dialog or motion to complete it, some require many lines and many motions to complete." Stanislavski paused to let this concept sink in before continuing.

Then, referring anonymously to his own work again he continued, "Let me give you another perspective. A great man once wrote that when an actor performs a play, he or she is actually moving through the story by moving through a series of intentions. Sometimes the intentions last for a single line within a single scene. Sometimes they take multiple scenes to complete. Each of the intentions is a beat in the play. The production is the connection of the intentions. To get from beginning to end, an actor must follow the line the intentions create, a line that leads through the story. The line runs from beat to beat through moment after moment." Stanislavski delivered this self reference with drama in his voice, clapping his hands on the first consonant of every word in the last sentence.

"I guess we all have our moments," the Product Manager added, clearly proud of his play on words.

"Yes," Stanislavski jumped back in, so completely absorbed in his teachings that he missed the attempt at humor entirely. "We do all have our moments. But, to pull those moments together, you need something."

Stanislavski walked slowly to the whiteboard on the other side of the conference room, opened a marker, drew a thick, horizontal line across the whiteboard and wrote two words on the board:

U N B R O K E N   L I N E

He capped the marker with a dramatic flare as if holstering a pistol after a successful shootout, and turned to the group.

There was silence in the room. As they had found themselves doing on numerous occasions with Stan, the staff waited for Stanislavski to explain himself. No explanation appeared forthcoming.

"An unbroken line?" The Communications Manager asked looking confused, an expression becoming more common with Stan in the room.

"Yes, an unbroken line. The unbroken line is the connection of the beats that takes you through the production process."

The Assistant Director half raised her hand in thought. "It's kind of like music, right? You have a verse, it lasts for a couple of bars, that's the end of a beat. Then there's the melody, the line of the music that takes you through the whole performance." She turned and looked at the group; her tone became somewhat indignant when all she encountered were blank stares. "What? I took piano as a kid," she muttered.

"Exactly," Stanislavski said with excitement in his voice, "Exactly. Now, a beat can be defined in different sorts of ways, perhaps it stretches from a moment where a character like Othello begins a conversation with his lieutenant Iago and ends a few minutes later when one set of motivations have run their course and the action needs to be redirected. Perhaps it just stretches from the first step out of a gondola to the second step, because the fundamental motivation of the stepper has changed between those two steps. You have to break apart a role to truly understand it."

"Boy," the Product Manager quipped, "I hope there's not a test on this Shakespeare stuff later."

"No, no test, just one point. You see, all of you, along with this company, are actors in the play we call the marketplace. It is the knowledge of our individual and corporate *self*, the understanding of the *actions* in behavior and our *observational skills* which empower us with the ability to connect with the character of our customers."

Stanislavski paused to let that sink in.

"That's a really interesting analogy, Stan," the Assistant Director responded after a few moments. "As we perform in the marketplace our actions have individual intentions which are individual beats."

The Communications Manager tentatively added another thought. "The customer has his or her own intentions and beats, too, right?"

It was the Assistant Director who addressed that issue. "Absolutely," she said with supreme confidence. "Our customers express many intentions, beats as you call them, during the course of any given day. They want to satisfy their hunger, they want shelter, they want to impress colleagues, they want to entertain elegantly, they want to show their spouse that they love him or her. It's endless."

"And we've seen the intentions and motivations of The Ater Company here," interjected the Product Manager, "They're all right here in the presentation." His voice trailed off as he realized the futility of his last ditch pitch to go back to the presentation.

"How do they come together?" asked Stanislavski.

The Product Manager chuckled, saying "That's the million dollar question, isn't it?"

"Actually," the Research Manager countered, "our annual revenues are significantly higher than that."

Stanislavski redirected the conversation back to this crucial point. "Be that as it may, a performer's job is to create an unbroken line of activity that connects the beats. That's our job here," he said, hopeful that he wasn't jeopardizing his identity by going too far with the analogy. He continued under the assumption that it had not been compromised. "A customer, as the main character in our production, follows his or her unbroken line of action throughout the course of the day. Where do our lines come together? Where do they intersect?"

"It's not just one place," the Assistant Director said.

"Yeah," added the Product Manager, "there's advertising, for instance. They see our brands on billboards and signs on the way to work. There's an intersection."

"Or, walking through a store, looking for a product," suggested the Research Manager.

Stanislavski agreed with their comments, but wanted to extract further insight from the discussion. "Take it to a more fundamental level. What is it about those intentions you mentioned, you know, hunger, love, shelter, what about those intentions require the resources and capabilities of our corporate *self*?"

After a moment of thought, the Assistant Director asked, "Stan, when you talk about beats, is it correct to assume that an individual cannot move on to the next beat until the current beat has been seen through to its conclusion?"

"Give me an example," Stanislavski pushed.

"Let's say the intention of my action is something basic, like, *to satisfy my hunger*. I'm looking for a restaurant, that's my primary intention. That intention has to either pass or something else has to happen to make it less relevant. Otherwise it continues in perpetuity."

"Correct. There has to be either a satisfactory resolution or abandonment of the current beat before moving on to the next beat."

"If that's true," she continued, "and the customer cannot move to the next beat until the current beat has been resolved or abandoned, then it seems logical to assume that they will continue to shop the market for someone who can satisfy their intention and close their beat, or will they withdraw from the market"

"Until then, I guess *the beat goes on.*" The Research Manager seemed to be singing the phrase, but Stan didn't get the reference. The others seemed to find it amusing so Stanislavski played along.

"Excellent!" proclaimed Stanislavski in a most dramatic voice. "You have hit upon the heart of the matter. Without satisfaction of intention, the show can't go on!"

"And, as we know," commented the Production Manager, "the show must go on."

Stanislavski picked up the pace of the conversation. "The question I now pose back to you is: What is the role of our corporate *self* in the customer's intention, or beat?"

Before anyone could answer, the Product Manager jumped in, "To provide the product necessary to complete the beat." He added a slight cadence to the sentence to emphasize the rhyme. "Hey, I'm a poet."

"But what if the beat's closure comes from a message as opposed to a product?" asked the Communications Manager. "Can messages complete beats?" she asked hopeful that communications would be included in the repertoire of beat closing actions.

"I think the point that Stan is making is that the completion of a beat, the satisfaction of an intention, can come from many sources," added the Assistant Director, "I would say that it is just as likely that a capability inside our self satisfies a beat as it is that a product satisfies the beat."

Stanislavski redirected the conversation back to the issue at hand for his team: that of how to connect the resources of The Ater Company's corporate *self* with the needs of its customers. "I think that you are all correct. As I see it, our job, or better yet our role in the marketplace, is to help see that the beats get closed, that our products are selected, and our production goes on. To do that, we must first identify the beats. Then, and only then, can we determine what would move the customer to completion of a given beat. With that knowledge we ask ourselves what we need to do to move the show along. Once we know that, we can dig within our *self* and identify a resource or capability to apply to the beat *to keep the show on the road.*"

"I guess we're all going to have to fall in line," quipped the Research Manager.

"Precisely!" exclaimed Stanislavski, clearly encouraged by the progress he was making. "We have to get in line with the customer. "

"I get this now," the Assistant Director said. "On the one hand, you could say that we here in marketing are the directors of this play. Our job is to identify the beats of the play and position our actor, namely the corporate *self*, in a position to help move the customer, our character, through the beats. But how do we do it?"

The Communications Manager had a suggestion. "Let's take this back to the beginning and look at the results of the audits."

The Research Manager handed out copies of the presentation and people started flipping through the sections on internal and external motivations.

"Ask yourself this question," Stanislavski suggested. "How can a department such as distribution contribute to the resolution of a beat? How does finance add a piece? And, how does the solution change *if*," he emphasized the if, "*if* a piece is added in one way as opposed to another?"

"So, if you've got a customer who's passing through a *beat of impatience* with the hassles of shopping," added the Assistant Director, "then on-line shopping or a virtual store, for example, can serve you."

The Product Manager continued, "When a customer's beat is convenience, distribution can add to the resolution through innovative delivery solutions through our regional wholesale network."

"So different types of customers experience different beats, but generally markets as a whole have similar beats," the Assistant Director said to no one in particular. "That's part of the issue we have to deal with. I guess that means that there are a number of lines out there for us both to stand in and to direct."

Stanislavski, standing throughout this entire conversation, walked over to the Research Manager's presentation. Does anyone have any tape?"

The Research Manager quickly darted out of the room, and reentered a few moments later with a roll of clear tape. "Here you are."

Stanislavski thanked him and began to tape individual slides containing statements of motivation and action, both of the corporate *self* and of the character of the customer, in a line.

The Assistant Director immediately understood what Stanislavski was doing. She walked over to the whiteboard and began to write on the overheads, much to the chagrin of the Research Manager. She began numbering them as individual beats, or moments, in the marketplace.

"So, this set of beats creates this line." She looked at it, pulled a few of the slides down, put up a few new ones, and reordered the group. "This set of beats forms this line. In a way, each line has its own personality. I guess we have to be true to the personality of the line, or our role doesn't fit. There are some personalities we can't really do," the Assistant Director added. "You can see it in this line here." She reassembled the overheads into a pattern with completely inconsistent internal and external motivations. "Here is a circumstance where we just don't fit with any of the beats."

So where then do the lines lead?" asked the Communications Manager. "What's the grand finale?"

"That is yet to come," Stanislavski said, somewhat obliquely to pique their interest. "There are other things we need to do in the interim to prepare for the finale. One part of that effort involves traditional market research," Stanislavski continued, "and, over the next few days, I'm going to teach you two other concepts that will help us decide which lines work and which ones don't. For now, I want to concentrate on what's possible. Later we'll focus on what's best for this company and our production."

They spent the remainder of the afternoon rearranging the pages on the wall, trying to find lines which connected appropriate resources to motivations. By the end of the session, they had a whole catalogue of possible connections between the internal *self* and the character of the customer.

* * * * * *

The nature of acting is that the actor knows the sequence of events of a performance and knows in advance how the character and story will develop. But, in order to give a convincing performance and be true to each moment of the performance, an actor is taught to identify what Stanislavski called *beats*. Each beat is a distinct point in the development of the character and the story, and each beat contains a specific objective for the actor involved in the action of the beat. The collective series of beats in a performance creates what is termed *the unbroken line*, which is defined by Stanislavski in metaphorical terms as a line which "flows from the past, through the present, into the future; from the moment you wake in the morning until you close your eyes at night." The unbroken line provides a central point of attention on which to focus action during a performance.

Connecting with customers is not the result of any one event or any one single function within a company. Making a connection with customers is the result of a marketing process which runs from the earliest stages of product development to the final stages of post-sale relationship management and hopefully follow-on sales. It is a continuum of beats that involves many individual players and settings. It is a melding of individual motivations and actions. All too often individuals focus only on individual manifestations of the process: sales, research, distribution, advertising, and more. What is often overlooked is the unbroken line of beats which takes a company from the early stages of marketing straight through to a successful exchange with the customer.

The difficult questions are how to choose which *lines* are best for a specific company and which *beats* support the objective of following a course down a particular *line*? That's the matter Stanislavski addresses in the next two chapters.

Scene VII

Emotion Memory

*The best story tellers make you feel the emotions
as they tell you the events of the story*

The best storyteller is the one that takes you along for the emotional ride as opposed to simply imparting a sequence of events. In the next scene, Stanislavski explains to his team that emotion plays a part in his method and explains how its memory plays an important role in marketing.

*　*　*　*　*　*　*　*

A few days after their discussion of the unbroken line, the marketing team found themselves together at a lunch to celebrate the retirement of a long-standing employee of The Ater Company. A majority of the senior staff was assembled to say good-bye to this man who, over the course of his forty-plus years with the company, had risen literally from the position of shop apprentice all the way to vice president of procurement. His ability to manage relationships with suppliers was widely known

114

throughout the company. The man was something of a corporate icon. There were pictures of him scattered throughout the hallways posing along side his colleagues and various members of senior management commemorating many of the company's important milestones. Even though the CEO was relatively new to the company he was sorry to have to preside over the departure of a person so rich in institutional value.

The marketing team took their seats around one of the tables set up in the cafeteria at The Ater Company's corporate headquarters and listened to the CEO offer a toast.

"These days you don't come across many people making this kind of long-term career commitment to a company," the CEO said. "I guess that's just the nature of the business world we've evolved into. What concerns me," he continued, "is that as people like our good friend here depart our daily company, we can't allow ourselves to lose the history of this company that he possesses. Sure, we need to make changes and we are making changes, but we can still learn from our past and we need to respect our corporate heritage."

The CEO turned to the man, raising his glass of water in a gesture. "I know I've learned a lot from him and I'll be calling him long after he's left to ask about the history of our vendor relationships. Thank-you for your commitment and we look forward to keeping you as part of our family."

The man stood up slowly and shook the CEO's outstretched hand. "Speech, speech," the calls came up from the crowd. Stanislavski clapped his hands together with the rest of the assembled audience, looking to draw the man's words from him.

After a few moments, the Retiring Man raised his hands to settle the crowd. "I'd ... like to thank you, all of you." It was clear he was holding back a tear and wasn't the sort of person accustomed to giving speeches in public. "It's been a great forty-some years here. I guess I've seen a lot of changes."

He took a sip of water and the group waited for him to continue. "When I started over forty years ago, we were a small fish in the big pond of our market. When I got out of high school it was a time of real turmoil in our country. I'm from a small town and apprentice was one of those jobs you wanted to get in the big city. I considered myself lucky to get the job and I felt fortunate to come to work here every day."

The assembled crowd was silently and intently listening to the man's speech seemingly hanging on his every word.

"Soon after I got my first promotion we followed the trend and moved some of the facilities out to the suburbs. There was so much new space being built and the old place was getting a bit rundown and musty. I was one of the first to move into the new shop. We started working on all of the offices, putting in the furniture for the executives. Then we had to get all the equipment in for the shop floor." He laughed for a moment. "Come to think of it, that seems a bit backwards. It was a complete mess for a few weeks. Fortunately for us, and thanks to the foresight of some smart execs, we had enough inventory and supplies to cover any drop in productivity. But then again, the market wasn't as demanding back then, you know, just in time delivery meant in the right month, not the right hour."

The Distribution Manager that Stanislavski had met on the first day called out from one of the tables nearby, "What do you mean, right hour? I want the right material from your suppliers at the right minute!"

"You're right, you're right," the Retiring Man said. "That all began twenty to thirty years ago, I guess. You know, the oil crisis, production dropped, we all thought we'd be out of a job. The Japanese were coming into the market and threatening our stranglehold on demand. And we were recovering from turmoil around the world."

More tears were welling up in his eyes, and the CEO reached over put his hand on the Retiring Man's shoulder. "Well, we kept going," he continued, "even with the troubles around the world, we were able to expand. We toughened up and bought a few good product lines just before the recovery; people were getting excited about what we could do."

"By that time, I was a manager managing some of our key supplier relationships," he continued. "I had meaningful work to accomplish and was working hard. In spite of that, I managed to find the time over the years to finish off my college degree and get a few graduate courses under my belt before taking on added responsibilities. A couple of additional promotions along the way and I've been in this position for over ten years now. It's hard to believe how time flies."

He stopped for a moment and looked around. He was clearly getting emotional. As he composed himself, his voice took on a much more confident and professorial tone. "The problems today, they're more than a sniffle, but they're not a disease. I know 'cause I've seen things like this before. This company's got a great heart, it's just that with all of the growth and contraction we've experienced lately this company needs to reevaluate where it's going and why. We've picked up and dropped off so much stuff in the past twenty years no one really knows what's here anymore. I'm a simple guy with lots of memories and few predictions. One thing I know for sure about the future, however, is that this company will always be a good company to work for even though I doubt any of you will beat my streak!"

People laughed and applauded, and the man sat back down to sip a newly poured cup of coffee. Stanislavski sat back, watched the man interact with his counterparts at the head table, and turned to his team.

He got their attention by asking, "What did you think of the speech?"

They all thought for a moment. "That's not the sort of speech you give a review of," the Assistant Director replied.

"My apologies," Stanislavski responded, "but I didn't mean it in terms of performance. I am more interested in terms of the content of the speech, what it says about our company and what we've been doing over the past couple of months in the marketing department."

"It says a lot about our corporate self," the Communications Manager said. "This company has been through a lot. So have the markets."

"But what has it been through?" Stanislavski pushed back against the response to see if his team could reach a deeper explanation.

"Lots of things," replied the Communications Manager. "I mean, I haven't been here for forty years, but it sounds like The Ater Company has definitely evolved and changed."

"How did he describe the changes?"

The Assistant Director picked up the line of questioning. "There were phases, individual time periods and sequences of events. Why?"

"Let's try to describe that progression differently," proposed Stanislavski. "Let's not talk about the memory of events but rather let's talk about the memory of emotions, or *emotion memory* as I call it."

"Emotion memory," repeated the Assistant Director. "Another one of your catch phrases, Stan?"

Stanislavski laughed inside. He had read in a humorous book about management theory that the key to directing company resources was to use meaningless catch phrases. So, the fact that they thought this was one of those catch phrases must have meant he had connected with his character, and was playing the role convincingly.

"Let me define emotion memory before we talk further about it. What's important to recognize, is that underlying his speech this man described emotions, not events. Sure, he listed events as he spoke, but that's not what he really said. Yes, he talked about moving to a new office. He spoke of expanding product lines. He told us about war time and about peace time. He grouped years into decades and he definitely listed a chronology of events." Stanislavski shifted forward in his chair to emphasize the point he was about to make. "But in a parallel way, the identical story can be told through the recounting of emotions; the progression from one emotion to the next throughout his career."

"So, for example, you start at the beginning," the Research Manager said. "There is the emotion of excitement and self-confidence then."

"But it's a small company, a small world," countered the Assistant Manager. "Confident might not be the right emotion to describe the company back then."

"Perhaps it's just something like, "comfortable," the Product Manager suggested.

"Let's say for now that it is some combination of the two," Stanislavski directed his staff. "Think about the discrete beats of the individual and of the company at that time and how, if at all, they were representative of the customers and markets. How did the emotions of the corporate *self* line-up with the external time and place?"

"If you look back in the economic data," the Research Manager said, "there were lots of smaller manufacturing and customer products companies back then. Many were located towards the center of towns, well connected to the communities. Like this one. At that time they weren't thinking of global markets, or even national ones for that matter."

"Companies thought regionally and locally," added the Assistant Director. "So did the customers."

"There's a line," the Product Manager realized. "The corporate self as comfortable and confident, the customers are closer to the brands and we're able to reach them."

"Is any of that relevant today?"

They thought it over for a while, until the Assistant Director ventured an answer. "I think part of it is. Many of our customers think about where we're from and what we support in the community. So, *comfortable with where we are and confident in our future*, I would say those are important."

"We've taken our first step in cataloging the emotion memory of this company."

"I get it," the Product Manager said. "You need to remember not just where you've been but also how you felt when you were there, so you can draw on those emotions to figure out how you would feel in the marketplace of similar circumstances. Wow, that hurt my brain."

"Absolutely," Stanislavski exclaimed in excitement over the connection that had been made to his method.

"Are we going to keep going?" asked the Product Manager. "If so, why don't we bring him over and ask him about the emotion memory of this company."

"A good idea." Stanislavski encouraged the Product Manager to invite the man over. Before he knew it, an additional five or six people were around the table talking, with the CEO listening intently at Stanislavski's side.

"The early days of my time here," added a woman executive, "which was almost thirty years ago, really combined a number of different emotions." "I showed up right at the end of the seventies, just when we were about to go through our first growing pains."

"But we only got there by tightening our belts," the Retiring Man commented. "We had to cut back the costs of all of our inputs so that we had some money to modernize. For a while, it was risky, but we signed a couple of key contracts with energy suppliers that set our fixed costs..."

"Afraid. Was that the emotion of the time?" interrupted the Research Manager, notebook in hand and pencil flashing down words on the page.

"Not quite," said the Retiring Man. "I'd say anxious, but it wasn't just us. Everyone was anxious. Compared to the steel people, for instance, we weren't afraid. Unlike them, we had some space to maneuver."

"The 1980s were a completely different story," the CFO said, introducing a new theme. "I was brought on near the end of the decade to help with acquisitions, and that wasn't confidence. That was more exuberance; deal after deal after deal we brought a lot of assets together in one company in what now seems like a relative short period of time. Exhausted, that's the emotion I remember most clearly."

"Everyone wanted us to be big," the Retiring Man said. "The CEO at that time," he continued, directing his comment to the present CEO, "he wanted growth. Everything was growth. We had teams to think about growth. Even I was on a growth team. That's when I got promoted again because I suggested a few good things they hadn't thought about."

"I'm surprised you weren't rewarded with early retirement," the Product Manager joked, a bit more gently than usual to make sure he didn't offend. The laugh from the Retiring Man made it clear that he did not take it personally. In fact, he used it as an opportunity to clarify his comments.

"There were a lot of people who wanted to move on. Said the company wasn't what it used to be. There was a touch of unrest in the emotional makeup of the company at that time."

The CEO ventured a comment. "Maybe the prevailing emotion was something like, excited but wary."

Events turned into emotions as literally two dozen people suggested various events and emotional patterns in the activities and personalities of individual people and the company as a whole. During the whole period, Stanislavski sat quietly, not really asking much but letting the conversation swirl around him. That was, until the CEO turned to him and said, "Stan, this is all very interesting, but what's the point of all of this?"

"I will answer that question with a question," he replied. "During all of those periods which we've been talking about, we have identified corporate emotions we were feeling. Is it fair to assume that the emotions we were feeling matched those of our markets?"

Everyone at the table deferred to the Retiring Man, "I think it is fair to say that we felt many of the same emotions within the company that were being felt by the markets and our customers. There were periods where consumer spending was high based on confidence in the economy, and there were times when consumer spending was tight based on anxiety over the economy. We've had times when concern for safety outweighed price points, and we've had times when consumers sought self esteem over frugality and quality. There have been a whole host of emotions in the markets, and I would say that more often than not we were swept up with them just like everyone else."

Before anyone could speak again, Stanislavski posed another question, "Have there ever been two distinct periods in the past forty plus years where sales have been up?"

Everyone assembled around the table shook their head and mumbled some sort of affirmative response.

"Now, during those two periods, was the fundamental emotion of the market the same?"

It was clear that Stanislavski was asking the Retiring Man so he answered saying, "I would say that actually there were many times when sales were up and confidence was high, and no, I wouldn't say that emotions were the same. I remember times when sales were up because of fear and times when sales were up because of high consumer confidence. We reacted differently in those cases."

"Exactly." That was all that Stanislavski said before turning his head to the Assistant Director.

Realizing that he expected her to take the discussion forward she looked back at him and said, "So what you're saying is that we should also evaluate events in the history of the markets and identify their emotional foundations. Is that right?" Stanislavski nodded, allowing her to continue. "And then we can match them together."

Stanislavski reached out to the notepad the Research Manager was using to keep track of the conversation. "These pages," he said, flipping through them one by one, "contain the emotional history of the company. These are opportunities, situations, and trends that might be relevant to today, or may present themselves tomorrow or next year. We've gotten to the point where we know what the techniques are for connecting our resources to the *character of the customer*, but we need to know what works and what doesn't. One of the tools for that is to go back into the past and apply the lessons of past experiences to present situations."

"Its best practices," the Research Manager said.

"Not really," countered the Assistant Director. "Best practices deal with discrete events or processes. We're talking about something more systemic."

"Exactly, it's the system," Stanislavski said with a bit of irony in his voice. "A system of remembering what your past emotional states are in given situations so that you can make them relevant to the existing production. Remember when we talked about work on one's self? This is work on one's self, but taken to a different level because it's helped us focus on choosing which beats and unbroken lines are going to be accepted by the customers and the market."

The marketing team had a pretty good idea of the implications of what Stanislavski was taking about, but the others at the table were shaking their heads, wondering exactly where the conversation was going. The Retiring Man was the first outsider to say anything.

"I understand what you're doing. You want to identify what we've felt around here and what was felt by the markets at specific times surrounding specific events so that you can draw on these emotions again when necessary. I'm all for bringing the best of the past into the present. But, even though I'm a man of the past around here ..."

"Not yet, you're not," the CEO interrupted. "I've got a few more contracts for you to look over."

"...even though I'm a man of the past," he continued, "I know that the future is more important. How are you planning to make choices based on the future? Are you also a fortune teller?"

Stanislavski smiled. "Yes, with emotion memory I can be a bit of a fortune teller. But that's between my staff and me. I've got a few weeks left to put together the marketing plan with my troupe; you don't want me to reveal everything right now, in front of my boss do you? In fact, I am hoping that even in retirement you will play a part in the production of our plan." The man agreed, not knowing what exactly he had just gotten himself into.

With that, the lunch broke up. The CEO walked over to Stanislavski, extended his hand and said, "I'm beginning to look forward to this presentation more and more."

"I'll want to rehearse it with you first," requested Stanislavski. "But there is one thing more left to teach to help my staff decide what the most important marketing directions are for this company. That's alignment. And that's next."

* * * * * *

There are a number of ways to describe an event or occurrence. One way, perhaps the most common, is to describe what happened in terms of a succession of actions, one following another in turn. Stanislavski suggests through his Method that, for an actor, it is sometimes better to describe an event in terms of the sequence of emotions that take place. The ability to identify the sequence of emotions driving a character through a scene is what Stanislavski calls the **emotional memory**. "The broader your emotional memory," Stanislavski once wrote, "the richer your material for inner creativity."

In marketing, it is critical to identify and understand the emotions and motivations which are at the core of marketplace events. Every consumer action and market trend is motivated by intentions which are based in emotion. By understanding the concept that actions are a means of expressing motivations and intentions, marketers can connect with the essence of buying behaviors. Once you connect with the underlying motivations of consumer behaviors you can use that knowledge to better perform your role on stage in the marketplace.

In the last scene, Stanislavski called upon his staff to broaden their emotional memories by translating events into emotions. The team defined a sequence of emotions and extrapolated what further capabilities would need to be taken into account in building The Ater Company's marketing strategy. Stanislavski drew the analogy between personal memory and institutional memory, and there's some thinking in both of those areas which may be of use to you before you move along to the next chapter:

On personal memory: Think of an event in your past.

- First, describe what happened in as much detail as you can remember, and put the sequence of events down in writing on the left side of a piece of paper.

- Then, on the right side of the piece of paper, connect events to emotions and feelings. Try to be as specific about each, phrasing it using Stanislavski's technique when possible (i.e., "I was nervous" might be better described as "I was overwhelmed by responsibilities and the implications of my actions").

- Finally, consider how you use each of these emotions and experiences to "give you perspective" when you encounter a new situation which might have a similar emotional foundation.

Now, apply the pattern to institutional memory. Think of an event in the history of a company. Describe the list of events, then look for motivations and actions behind each of the events, and consider how those "emotions" offer a base of reference for addressing problems.

Finally, apply the pattern to market memory. Think of an event that occurred in the marketplace; one as complex as a paradigm shift in consumer behavior or as simple as a customer choosing to purchase your product. Describe the list of events, then look for motivations and actions behind each of the events, and consider how those *emotions* offer a base of resources for addressing problems.

That base of resources can be used as a criterion for deciding what is possible for an institution to do and what is not. If the company has never experienced a period of extended change through expansion, for example, then there will be particular challenges in ensuring the organization can make it through such a transition.

From a marketing perspective, if a company has never reached a particular audience or connected with the marketplace in a certain way, it will be difficult but certainly not impossible to reposition the company toward the unknown without adding new emotion memories into the mix from which to draw guidance or inspiration.

But don't take this the wrong way. Just because you haven't ever done something doesn't mean you can't do it in the future. The point Stanislavski is trying to make is that as you develop a strategy to connect with existing or new customers you have to be able to draw on past emotion memories to identify connections with your objectives. If you don't possess the memory yourself, you need to find a way to acquire the memory so that you can apply it to your challenge.

But as with all good productions, things need to come together at the end. As you will see in the next chapter, there are additional elements of Stanislavski's method that can be used as a guiding criterion for choosing certain lines and beats over others. The next principal to be addressed is the concept of *alignment*.

Scene VIII

Alignment

Staying on track

Stanislavski tries to keep things on track in the next scene, where he mixes a bit of teaching with an unexpected outing to see one of his favorite productions at a local community theater.

* * * * * * * *

More than two months had passed since Stanislavski began his work with The Ater Company. His assignment had included developing a comprehensive marketing approach and plan for the company to use in the months and years ahead, so the pressure was on as the team faced their final deadline only two weeks away. The team had been working long hours using Stan's seemingly crazy concepts to develop both a plan and an approach that are centered on connecting the company with the character of the customer. They needed to find a way to effectively communicate their ideas to the directors and senior management committee at the end of the month.

129

One night, after a long afternoon of work on testing specific customer and company motivation scenarios, the Assistant Director came up with an idea she thought might defuse the tension; the group would go to the local community theater to see a production of Othello. She knew how much Stan enjoyed acting analogies and Shakespeare, so she figured it would be a good team building exercise. The next day, after consulting the others in the marketing team, she purchased tickets for an evening performance and surprised Stan with a ticket when he returned from lunch.

"I thought you'd appreciate the chance to see this troupe," she told him. "I hear they are very good for an amateur company."

Stanislavski smiled as he caressed the ticket. "I'm looking forward to this performance," he said. What she didn't realize was that he would be using the opportunity to introduce a final concept from his method.

That afternoon, the team left work a bit early and met up at the theater just before curtain time. A few minutes later they were seated in the middle of the theater just ten rows back from the stage when he curtain rose and the production of Othello began. This was one of Stanislavski's favorite productions, and he knew the entire play backwards and forwards. The Assistant Director noticed it immediately in Stan's facial expressions, especially during the sequences in the first part of the play where Othello stands up to the leaders of Venice by professing his love for Desdimona and effectively demanding recognition of that love before agreeing to fight for them once more.

The first act of the play came to a close and the group filed out of the theater and into the foyer to stretch. The managers ordered a few drinks at the bar and talked quietly amongst themselves about the show, though Stan was notably, and quite unusually, quiet.

The Assistant Director was a bit concerned that perhaps Stan wasn't enjoying the show. "What do you think, Stan? You seem quiet. Do you not like the production so far?"

"No, not at all. Quite the contrary, I like it very much. A few very effective performances so far, and I am interested to see how it will end."

The Assistant Director laughed. "Stan, you know how it is going to end. You love this story. In fact, you're mouthing the lines from your seat!"

The rest of the team had joined the conversation and each one smiled at the comment along with Stanislavski. "You're right," he said, "I know how the *script* is going to end, but I don't know how the *play* is going to end." His emphasis on script and play were quite deliberate and noticeable. "The production of a play is generally different from the script, especially in a situation like this. They're not doing all of Othello, for instance, it's been edited a bit. Some creative license is being taken by the director. Not all of the stage directions are the same for this production as they were with the original production. In every production the emotions are portrayed differently so different feelings are transferred from the actors to the audience. Because there are differences, you don't necessarily know how this play is going to end for *you*, even though the end of the story will not change." His emphasis again resonated with the managers as deliberate.

"Keeps it exciting," the Product Manager said for lack of anything better to offer.

"Yes, yes it does," Stanislavski agreed, "but, you see, there are parameters which should guide a company like this one in deciding what the specific end of this play is going to be. It's not a 'free for all' as they say. That is what interests me, because they have made some choices about characters and plot that might be considered, shall we say, non traditional."

They all looked at each other, not entirely sure of Stan's meaning. "I don't think any of us knows Shakespeare well enough to understand what those choices are," the Assistant Director responded for the group.

They had taken the bait and Stanislavski seized the opportunity. "Apply it to us for a moment," he began. "We're in the middle of interpreting what our customers intentions are, what their motivations are, and how we can build relationships with them in the play we call the customer in the marketplace. The important thing to remember is that in our case we're not writing the script of the play, the customer is."

"But we've got a part," the Research Manager objected.

"Well, yes and no," replied Stanislavski. "Actually, the customer is the character and we are the actor, so yes, we have a part but in many respects they are playing the part. Maybe a good way to put it is that we are the understudy. We need to be able to step in at a moment's notice and be as good at playing the part as they are." If the managers had previously thought they were on a break from Stan-isms by virtue of being out to the theater, they suddenly realized they were wrong.

Without regard for their confusion, Stanislavski pushed on. "We need to understand how to play the part according to the playwright's assignment and, in this case, the customer is also the playwright. The marketplace makes decisions about how the final drama is played out. For instance, do you choose the borscht, or the Reuben sandwich? Do you walk away down the street to a Chinese food place instead of the St. Petersburger deli? The similarity between Othello and our production is that the ending is written but the path to the conclusion will be different with each production. In our production, the ending is a successful transaction with our customer. The story feels different because each time there is a different actor playing the character, that of the customer."

Stanislavski took a sip of the diet cola he was drinking and continued. "For these actors and the director on stage, the goal is to interpret the words and ideas of the playwright. You read the script, you find out as much about the time in which the play was written and about the sources of information used by the playwright, all to bring together an effective performance. A director can edit, change parts of the scene, change furniture, even change the time and place when the play takes place, but, in my view, should not and cannot go against the intentions of the playwright."

Stanislavski concluded his thought with a summary statement: "Actions and directions must be in alignment with the intentions of the playwright."

The team thought about the comments for a moment. "You know, Stan," the Assistant Director commented, "we've been working with this analogy of the corporate *self* as an actor with marketing as a director who sets the stage and clarifies the motivations of individual players. We should take this idea to heart, and figure out what alignment with the intentions of the customer's script really means."

"Exactly my thought," agreed Stanislavski. He could see that she was beginning to subconsciously assimilate his method into her thinking.

The Communications Manager posed a question: "Is this like emotion memory? You know, describing the events of a play and finding out the emotions under the surface..."

"I'd like you all to think about alignment in a different way," Stanislavski responded. "Let's look at it in terms of this play, what's left of it, anyway."

"Shakespeare is building to a tragic ending, one filled with pathos and irony," Stanislavski began. "Othello is being betrayed by a man whom, at this point in the play, he trusts almost implicitly. It would be wrong for a director, for instance, to choose to change the ending of the play to reflect a happy ending. While it has been done before, I disagree wholeheartedly with the approach."

"It certainly would not be appropriate for The Ater Company, in any case," the Assistant Director commented. "We need to go where our customers want us to go. If we show up where our playwrights don't want us, that causes all sorts of problems."

Stanislavski agreed. "Correct. We have our exits and entrances in the play scripted by a customer and a market."

"Stan," the Assistant Director continued, "let's keep running with the acting analogy again."

"Considering how often I use the acting analogy," Stanislavski joked, "that's likely to be a marathon."

The Assistant Director smiled and addressed her question: "I wonder if there's a specific criterion that an actor or director uses for ensuring alignment with a playwright's intentions?"

"You have to search for it in two places: in the play, but also in the soul of the actor," Stanislavski responded, "which, in this case, refers to the play in the marketplace and the soul of the *corporate self* we have been talking about."

"This is the synthesis you've been talking about," said the Assistant Director. "You synthesize the external intention expressed in the play and the internal motivation and emotion memory of the actor into an actual production."

"Yes, yes," Stanislavski said, "that's exactly where we are heading. But, before we get there, let me introduce another idea which is meant to help us reach that synthesis. Alignment depends on defining a *supreme objective* for the production we call the competitive marketplace."

The blank looks on the face of his team indicated that he just boldly went where none of them had gone before.

"Let me give you an example of a supreme objective that you might consider part of the production: I wish to grow rich!"

"That's an objective I can relate to," interjected the Product Manager.

Stanislavski barely noticed the interruption and continued with his point. "Think of the variety of subtle motives, methods and concepts you can put into the idea of wealth and attainment. There is so much that the problem requires more than just one type of analysis; it requires a synthesis of all the different external and internal perspectives."

"If you are an actor, looking at this play," Stanislavski digressed for a moment, "the supreme objective of the story could be viewed in a number of ways, but it's a lot richer than just, *I want to be rich* or, *betrayal is a terrible thing.* But defining the supreme objective at the heart of the action requires a continual search for the truth in our *selves* and the truth of human experience being elaborated by the playwright."

"Let me get this straight," the Communications Manager said, with a very skeptical tone in her voice. "You expect us to be able to read the complexities of the market, the script as you say, and find a supreme objective? People have been trying to explain the world since the beginning of time, and we've gotten no closer."

"There, I think you're wrong," Stanislavski countered. "We the company must have read the world correctly in some way, or we wouldn't be in business at all. The supreme objective is, in part, already expressed in what we do. It emerges from the activities of the company."

"Maybe you don't simply state the supreme objective and move on," the Assistant Director said. "It's something you continuously work towards."

"That's my point exactly," Stanislavski said excitedly as he continued her line of thought. "It's is an ongoing conversation with other actors, with the playwright, whether directly or indirectly through the script and other writings. It is a continual search through who we are and what we will become."

The idea intrigued the Assistant Director, who took Stanislavski's point one step further. "And we've already done it, at least a part of it. You remember the conversations we started, back when you asked us to define action and motivation?"

"Yes," Stanislavski responded.

"That's what we need to keep doing. The *supreme objective* of our customers' actions emerges out of the continuous conversations, out of the dialogue between our people, our customers, and others playing a role in the activities of the marketplace."

"How can we use this in our marketing plan?" asked the Research Manager.

"Yeah, it sounds like part of the criterion of choosing which lines work and which don't," added the Product Manager.

The Assistant Manager responded for Stanislavski. "We do so by formalizing the conversation about the supreme objective. We pursue our quest for the supreme objective by making it a part of our every day activities in the marketing department, and throughout the company."

"Sounds like the theme for a great Monty Python movie," said the Research Manager.

"Since unlike a finished play, we don't already have an exact script, but we do have an ending in mind. The *supreme objective* of *our* script is ever changing and evolving but it leads toward the purchase of our products and services. The ongoing conversations we have, and the process of reading and re-reading the script as it changes, both help the supreme objective emerge from the actions of the customers and the market," Stanislavski added.

"That is what this company should be aspiring to," the Assistant Director concluded. "Alignment through ongoing dialogue about the motivations, actions and the objectives of the characters with whom we are connecting."

The team paused to sip their drinks and consider the point. The lights dimmed then came back to full power, signaling the play was going to start again in a few moments.

"Fascinating," said the Assistant Director. "The scope of the idea is fascinating."

"One thing we can say for sure," said the Research Manager said, again ingratiating himself, "Stan Islavski's method works."

The man behind the bar leaned into the conversation but only Stan was standing close enough to hear over the noise in the hall. "Of course, Stanislavski's method works," the bartender said. "I'm a part-time actor and I've read all of his books. In fact, I've got a copy of one right here with his picture on the back of it."

"I'm sorry we won't be able to take a look," Stanislavski said quickly without turning to face the man behind the bar. Hoping that his cover wasn't completely blown by this interruption he directed the managers back to the theater saying, "The second act is about to begin."

He pressed his colleagues towards the door before the bartender could return with his book.

"Now the challenge is to sell the CEO and the board on all of these ideas," the Assistant Director said to Stanislavski as they re-entered the theater.

Stanislavski gestured expansively, saying, "It will require a combination of theatrics and good thinking combined with effective preparation and of course, a good rehearsal. But let's worry about that tomorrow. The play is about to resume, and I can't wait to see how it ends."

* * ** * *

Stanislavski believed that a truly successful performance is one in which the action of the actor is aligned with the intentions of the playwright. The playwright presents to the cast a set of circumstances with a fixed path from beginning to end. Some of the circumstances are subject to adaptation by the director and actors while others are essential to the characters, the plot and the course of events. An actor must understand the intention of the playwright and understand how to adapt the action of the characters to match that intention thereby transporting the character through the unbroken line from beginning to end. To stay aligned with the intention of the playwright, Stanislavski taught his actors to ask question like "how does a specific condition or action affect the goals and objectives of the playwright?" or "what can we do to set our objectives to ensure we direct our actions appropriately?"

Marketing and communications professionals have a fundamental responsibility to ask the same questions about their actions relative to aligning the mission and direction of a company with the script of the marketplace. Every customer and market has strategic objectives and goals to achieve. Those objectives can be explicitly stated or implicitly displayed by their choice of products or markets. Marketing has a responsibility to keep the company 'on track' and in alignment with the goals and objectives of the script that is being written and played out by playwrights in the marketplace.

The key point in this story is this: alignment is only possible through ongoing conversation and dialogue about objectives, motivation and action. This is more of what Stanislavski calls "work on one's self," but it has particular meaning for businesses trying to follow the script of the marketplace to conclusion. Individual management practices for functions like marketing, communications, operations and finance all need to be based on sustaining the conversations that allow the supreme objective of marketplace activity to be identified, respected and acted upon.

Stanislavski's method has given his team a start, initiating conversations within and outside the company about what the future direction of the market is and how individual customers will write the next chapter of the drama of marketplace competition. But Stanislavski needs to show more than just the conversation, he needs to show the implications of the conversation. That final challenge is the focus on the last two chapters.

Scene IX:

A Good Rehearsal

Practice really does make perfect

Many actors will tell you that a bad rehearsal the night before a show opens is a good omen. Stanislavski disagreed. Stanislavski believed that rehearsal was a time to grow, not just practice. In the next scene, Stan explains to the CEO the importance of good rehearsals.

* * * * * * * *

The Assistant Director smiled at Stanislavski from the hallway as he stepped onto the elevator to head up to the CEO's office. "Stan, just remember," she said in a disarming and concerned tone, "you're market testing the marketing plan. This talk about rehearsing, well, it's interesting, but that's not really what you're doing here."

Stanislavski stepped back out of the elevator into the hallway and let the doors close behind him. He had a few minutes before his scheduled appointment and he wanted to take a moment to address the issue raised by the Assistant Director.

"I know," Stanislavski responded, "that during our last few meetings I have been emphasizing the need to *rehearse* parts of our *performance* by making sure that the people we've interviewed and the people who have helped us develop this plan are a part of the final production."

The Assistant Director sighed, readying herself for another of what they now referred to amongst themselves as *Stan-isms*.

"When I say rehearse, I don't mean to just walk through the presentation, I mean to further develop upon and build the synthesis between ourselves and the characters we are developing. You see, the way I see it, a rehearsal is meant to be an exchange of ideas."

"You've said that before, Stan."

"Yes, but I don't think I have made myself entirely clear. The best rehearsals are the ones where you learn something new about your role as a player within the company, as a member of the group responsible for the performance. It's a practice for sure, but it's really a growth experience."

"This goes back to the point you made about alignment," the Assistant Director said, building on her point, "Keep the internal and external conversations going to make sure the company is aligned with the intentions of its customers."

"That's right, but there's something I haven't said yet. You see, rehearsal is about interaction and experimentation. True rehearsals can only happen in an open, honest atmosphere."

The Assistant Director thought about that for a moment.

"From what I understand about the corporate world today," Stanislavski added, "there's precious little of that around. When you can find it, you should nurture it."

Stanislavski hit the button on the wall and called for the elevator to return. "I'm not looking just to market test the marketing plan," he said as he heard the elevator approaching. "I'm looking to lay the ground work for an environment that will allow us to share ideas before and after the big performance is over and done with."

The elevator arrived and he stepped back through the doorway. As the doors closed, he added, "Who knows? I expect that someday soon you will be the director of your own production, responsible for demonstrating the same sort of leadership."

Before she could comment further, the doors closed and Stanislavski began his ride to the executive suites in the building. He took a moment to remember the main points he was going to make, but he also knew he had to fulfill an agenda that the Assistant Director and the others on his team were not aware of.

He had to justify his performance in the role of Director of Marketing to the man who cast him in that role.

The elevator bell dinged once as the door opened. Stanislavski turned to the right, entered through another familiar set of doors, and arrived at the CEO's office.

"He's expecting you," the secretary said as she gestured toward the CEO's office. She was in on the plot of the CEO. It had taken her a bit of time to forgive "Stan" for his behavior the first time they met but the man and the character were both beginning to grow on her and she would be sorry to see his time at the company come to a conclusion.

"Mister Director," the CEO expounded broadly as Stanislavski entered the room. "My, my, you have become your character." The two shook hands in the center of the office. "Yes," the CEO continued, "you even look the part. You've come a long way from the theater to the boardroom."

"Thanks, how is your day going?" asked Stanislavski, continuing the lighter tone of the conversation.

"Always busy," the CEO said grimly, but still with a smile on his face. "At least I don't have your job, though. All I've got to do is manage this production. Hey, I guess that makes me a producer," he added with a wink and a smirk.

"Why don't you have a seat," the CEO said, gesturing to the chair. He walked around the desk to his own seat, and asked, "You need a cup of coffee or something?"

"Are you having anything?"

"Sure am. These morning meetings just don't work without a good cup of coffee." He walked over to the bar that was in his office and poured two cups of coffee.

"How's the final performance shaping up, Constantin? Your presentation is at the end of the week."

"Tomorrow I meet with the rest of the cast..."

"I think you mean to say team," the CEO interrupted.

"Funny, I'm still having trouble with a bit of the terminology. But in this case I do mean cast. You'll see. I meet with them tomorrow to review their parts in the big presentation. We'll make changes then and be ready for the end of the week."

"You're here to give me a preview, I assume."

"Actually, I'm here to rehearse," Stanislavski responded.

The CEO chuckled. "You don't have to use the acting analogies with me, Constantin, I know what we're up to here."

Stanislavski smiled knowingly saying, "Maybe, maybe not. Let's start from the beginning and let me take you through how this role of Marketing Director that you've cast me in has evolved. That way, when we get to the final performance, you'll understand how I play the role a bit better."

It was the CEO's turn to smile knowingly. "You're playing the consultant's trick on me. You want to tell me how you've done what you've done before telling me what you've done. Smart, very smart."

The CEO stood up, walked over to the cabinet and opened the doors to his whiteboard. The three objectives they discussed during his interview were still there, just as they were after he had written them.

"I know what you're thinking," the CEO smiled. "Did he write these out before I showed up, or have they been sitting there for the past three months? To be honest, this is the first time I've used the whiteboard,

I thought it was a neat toy for the office, but I'm used to having my meetings over in the conference room."

They both laughed at the point, but the look on the CEO's face indicated that it was time to get down to business. "The first point was: *understand the competencies and resources of the business*. What has been done on that front?"

"We started by focusing on three concepts," Stanislavski replied. "First was *work on one's self*, second was *action* and third was *motivation*. Our goal was not only to employ the acting technique in an attempt to define the competencies and resources of the business, but also to introduce a discipline for how to describe those competencies and resources."

"Give me a for instance, Constantin."

"In the marketing department, we no longer understand our motivations as something vague, like, being the market leader. These days we define them specifically - more along the lines of, *to make our customers feel secure*. We initiated a discussion within the company about how employees view the business and their own contributions to it. What we got was an interesting mix, a real view of our value chain."

"What did you do next?"

"Magic," Stanislavski replied, playing with his facial expression in a childlike manner.

That seemed to work with the CEO. "You're sounding more and more like a consultant each day, willing to take credit but not willing to specify the process." The CEO returned to more serious business, pointing to the second bullet: *understand our customers and the motivators of customer behaviors*. Where do we stand on that one? Tell me what you've done."

"We started addressing the external challenges with observation, and then we moved into what I guess a real consultant would call scenario planning, role playing in other words, talking about what might happen at a particular moment of sale and asking the *team*," he emphasized the word team to make the point that he had fixed the earlier misstatement, "to think about the specific circumstances of our customers. We spoke with one of our key customers, talked a lot about his concerns, issues and the ways in which he assessed our value. Then we went to visit other customers and prospective customers and we asked a lot of 'if' questions about what we're doing, what me might do, and how they would react to it. We also asked ourselves *what if we were them* types of questions."

"I remember that, we were at the deli together and you were talking about that stuff; describing customer actions in terms of motivations and intentions."

"Exactly." Stanislavski punctuated his comment with a raised finger and an emphasis on the second syllable of the word. Upon reflection, he thought it was a bit of over-acting, but the CEO had already moved on to the next point.

"That's all well and good, Constantin, but how does all of that line up?"

"Its interesting that you'd use that colloquialism, to *line it up*. That's exactly what we did. We sketched out a set of unbroken lines that are likely to lead our customers through the beats of their everyday routine directly to our products and services."

The CEO nodded, understanding more than Stanislavski expected from that particular description. He jumped ahead in the conversation. "How many of these lines are there? And how profitable would each of them be?"

"You'll see all of those," came the response. "You've given me a Research Manager who can bind up all of these conversations and put color graphics in them that even I don't understand."

"I'm sure they'll all look very impressive and that it will take us a few weeks to pour over them," the CEO responded, "but that's not going to impress me half as much as you trying to explain how you've gotten to this third point: *Defining the implementation process for marketing and communications.*"

"The implementation process," Stanislavski began, "depends on two things: the past and the future."

"What?"

"You saw the past in our conversation at that retirement luncheon where you gave the speech. The past is our *emotion memory*. We look to the past and see what works, what doesn't work and how we felt during certain moments."

"So what about the future?" asked the CEO.

"That's *alignment* and it involves constantly talking with our customers and our employees to ensure that we're still on the right track with our messages, product development, all of that marketing stuff. That ongoing conversation leads us to the tactical choices we make on implementation."

The CEO picked up his pen and, in a thoughtful way, drew a slash through each of the three bullets, indicating the contract had been fulfilled.

"Let's think past this presentation," the CEO said, "because you and I both know it's not the end product of this specific presentation that matters here but rather, it's the continuation of your method as a process that will be our collective legacy."

"That's what I mean about this being a rehearsal," Stanislavski said, clearly surprising the CEO. Before the CEO could ask for an explanation, Stanislavski offered one.

"You see," Stanislavski began, "for an actor, no performance ever really ends. What you do with each role and the experiences you have off stage all become part of your emotion memory. As an actor you are constantly working on your *self*, trying to draw an unbroken line from your own intentions and capabilities to the needs and interests of the character you are playing on stage. While the rehearsal is about the performance, it is really a forum for the exchange of ideas. But more importantly, it is a chance to try out different techniques and to apply different elements of your *self* to your role and see what fits best. Rehearsal is an opportunity to revisit material you are familiar with and rethink how to apply the self you are at the time to the role you're playing and how to take from that performance to improve your next performance, even before it starts."

"What you're telling me," the CEO said, "is that you actually came in here to talk to me about next steps, not about the presentation."

"Correct. The key is in the nature of the long-term synthesis that you and others bring to this company." Stanislavski brought out the dramatic training for the first time in the conversation, raising the tenor of his voice slightly and taking on the persona of a leading role in an important moment of a storyline. "For an actor, the synthesis comes from the moment when you are actually on stage, acting, pulling together what you are with what you perceive the character should be. At that point the actor knows what he can do and the actor knows the character. Synthesis comes from acting itself; it comes from being on stage as the character, in relation to other characters and the audience watching the performance. Synthesis is in essence a convincing performance."

"What makes a convincing performance? When does synthesis occurs?" pressed the CEO. "And based on whose experience, the actor or the audience?"

"A true portrayal of the character communicates the authenticity of the performance," Stanislavski said with confidence. "It is what makes the audience accept the actor as the character, and what makes the actor understand the character is in alignment with the truth inside of his self."

"So, the actor knows that he or she has successfully mastered the role when the audience accepts the character?"

"Actually no, it's quite the contrary. In my method the audience's acceptance is irrelevant. The criterion for successful synthesis comes from inside the actor. My method says that true synthesis comes when the actor, and only the actor, from inside, realizes the truth in what is being acted upon on stage."

"It doesn't matter whether the audience accepts his portrayal?"

"In the strictest sense, that is correct."

The CEO thought about it for a second. "It sounds to me like the difference between doing art for art's sake, and doing art to please a specific audience."

"You might say it that way," Stanislavski mused. "I know that acting is a business but true performance comes from truth to character, not truth to audience."

"Your first answer is a problem." The CEO put down the marker for the whiteboard and crossed to glance out of the window behind his desk. "This company plays for an audience, we don't play for ourselves. The criterion of success in the world of profit and loss is acceptance of our performance, our products and services, by the audience of customers." The CEO was accustomed to intellectual sparring but this was making his head spin. He suddenly felt a twinge of sympathy for the marketing team but that passed quickly as Stanislavski tried to address his concern.

"I know," replied Stanislavski, "and I know that a play will close if the audience doesn't accept it." He turned to look out the window obviously consumed by the conversation and his own thoughts. With his back turned to the CEO he continued, "Think about it this way, if you can not accept the character in yourself, how can you expect others to believe the character you are presenting in the marketplace? *Synthesis* is the result of the successful application of my method." He turned back to face the CEO seeming more confident in his thoughts. "The rehearsal allows you to make a link between your own acceptance of the character and the presentation of that character to an audience. The rehearsal is the time when we get together and practice applying our self to the part, independent of acceptance, using all of the tools of the method. Rehearsal is how we come together to search for expansion and improvement."

The CEO took a step toward Stanislavski and said, "I know about rehearsals, I've been in a few. You tell people where to go and when to move in what way."

"No, now you are blocking me," replied Stanislavski.

Before he could continue, the CEO apologized with a quick, "Sorry, Constantin," and took a step to the left of the whiteboard.

"No, not that blocking, I mean blocking my scene. You know, what the director does to direct the actors. In an original production, the director moves the players around until he finds a place where each one fits and is aligned with the action of the scene. But you could also say that you are blocking me with your questions. You're using them to tell me where and how to move in my thinking."

"I see what you are saying," replied the CEO. "Dialogue is the intellectual equivalent of blocking. We're talking to each other, exploring the environment in which we are going to play. We're improvising, planning how to build a relationship with the audience which will crescendo into an exchange of acceptance."

The CEO took a breath, his face registering recognition of the importance of a good rehearsal. "I guess I need to be more aware of how actions and comments can be mistaken for blocking directions. If I'm not careful I could inadvertently *block* a scene in our production, for lack of a better term, that either inhibits or prohibits synthesis because I have put our character in the wrong place at the wrong time."

"Maybe we need more blocking and tackling drills around here," Stanislavski said unexpectedly. He had heard someone use that term at a meeting at some point and just blurted it thinking it might apply here. The CEO laughed.

After composing himself he continued. "There are numerous blocking techniques we use as directors to communicate with the audience. There is voice, body language, then there is staging, sets, lights, props, all of those elements are part of the method."

"Yeah, and many of them we can use here," replied the CEO. "I think I'm getting it. You position bodies and voices, we position products and communication messages. We use dialog and direction internally but we use distribution and communications externally. We study the blocking of our character, the customer, as they act out their part in the marketplace production so we can block ourselves to be in the right place at the right time when they act."

"That's very good," offered Stanislavski. "But don't forget that blocking is a mechanical function. Don't forget that to achieve synthesis you have to center on the actor and the director. For now, I am the director, and we are preparing to connect with the character of our customer in the marketplace. Soon I will be handing this production over to someone new and the challenge will be to continue to use my method as the company and its cast encounters new characters, new customers, new scripts and new markets with which to connect."

"Speaking of which," the CEO said as he rose from his chair, "how is your protégé coming along in her training?"

"The Assistant Director? Very well, and I made the same point to her this morning. The heart of it is a certain kind of leadership, one appropriate to a rehearsal. My hope is that, more than just finishing my assignment and working through the contract specifications, I've been able to help set a standard as a Director in this company."

"Well, that's what I'm paying you for," the CEO said with a bit of an edge in his voice. Stanislavski thought to himself that perhaps he had overplayed his hand and offended the CEO, but the next comment from his employer was much softer.

"You've got two more days to be our director. Go rehearse. Do what you need to do to bring our little *production* to life."

Stanislavski smiled as he left the room, knowing that this rehearsal had been a success. Now all he had to do was make sure his actors all had their lines and roles memorized for the upcoming performance.

* * * * * *

Rehearsals happen on a daily basis. The question is, *what makes a good rehearsal for an actor*? Stanislavski taught his students that rehearsal time, while being partially a technical exercise in blocking and dialogue, was an opportunity to come together in an effort to exchange and share ideas. No performance happens spontaneously or opens the day after casting. A production is the result of individual efforts brought together interactively through rehearsal. Rehearsal is the time for all of the players to find their place in the performance and understand where they fit into the bigger picture.

Above all, Stanislavski used rehearsal as an opportunity to exchange and share ideas and techniques. It was a time to think about the broader issues and then apply them in very specific and rigorous ways to the particular demands of the performance at hand.

The scene we've just gone through has to do both with marketing and the nature of the corporate environment. In the scene with the CEO, Stanislavski is arguing that without an environment based on honest, open leadership and free flowing dialog, no rehearsal can occur. His argument is that not having regular *rehearsals* will ultimately limit the effectiveness of any marketing method.

But, as Stanislavski would argue, no company rehearses just for the sake of rehearsing and no company can afford to just rehearse and not take steps to serve the needs of its customers. The production's the thing, and Stanislavski's new acting company's performance begins in the next chapter.

Feel free at this point to take a brief intermission, stretch your legs, freshen up your drink and refill your popcorn. But remember, when the lights flash its time to return to your seats for the big production.

Scene X:

The Performance

Bringing the Method to life

The finale of our story involves a meeting, a performance and a confession through which Stanislavski and his staff employ their own cast of characters to bring their version of method marketing to life.

* * * * * * * *

Stanislavski and his team entered the board room quietly, carrying nothing but their thoughts. Thanks to the Research Manager all of the equipment was in place and the materials were loaded on the server and ready to go. The room was empty. The presentation on the future marketing direction of the company was first on the morning agenda. They had a few minutes to prepare before everyone arrived.

As the Research Manager double checked everything and helped the technician get the projection system ready, Stanislavski felt at home for the first time in three months. He was about to go on stage. He would be performing for a small, but select audience. The meeting was being held in the company's training room which had several rows of tables with chairs and a small dais at the front. It was unusual for such a meeting to take place in this room but the setting fit their need so the CEO had accommodated the request.

"The stage is set," Stanislavski said out loud but to no one in particular.

Aside from his staff, there were a few guest who were going to join with him in the presentation; *extras* is how he had jokingly referred to them the day before, each playing a role that had been rehearsed the afternoon before. First, there was the Chief Financial Officer, who, after seeing the results of the internal and customer surveys, not only revised some of his thinking on the pricing strategy, he also changed his investor presentation to reflect his new thinking about his role in the company. The Distribution Manager had a few lines in the second act about aligning the resources of his staff with those of the sales departments. And, in the climatic moments of the third act, other voices would join the chorus, including the now-retired Retiring Man. In addition, the Customer with whom the team had spoken in their conversations about the magic "if" agreed to join the play. He brought along his Purchasing Manager whom he referred to as his supporting cast.

Finally, there was the Shopper whom Stanislavski had found walking the aisles in one of the Customer's stores during his search for customer motivation and behaviors. She happily sat over in the corner, drinking a cup of tea and speaking with the Customer in an animated fashion.

"Finally," Stanislavski said to himself as he saw all of the players assembled in front of him, "I get to be a real director again."

The Customer broke from his conversation with the Shopper and approached Stanislavski, hand extended. "I'm glad that we finally get the chance to meet. I like the work you've done here. I'd like to teach it to the managers at my company. Let's be sure to stay in touch."

"I'd be glad to and I'm glad that you are able to join us," Stanislavski replied politely.

"Like I said, if one of the action-hero Hollywood types isn't available, I'll just have to put in a cameo appearance and play myself."

The Chief Financial Officer put his hand on Stanislavski's shoulder and asked, "Are you sure it's all right for me to join you for this? You realize you've got a limited amount of time with these people, probably no more than forty-five minutes or so."

"What is drama without other players?" Stanislavski smiled back broadly, realizing the Chief Financial Officer's participation lent significant credibility to the production. "Besides, marquee names always help an opening," he bantered back. "I am glad we'll get to play on the same stage together."

The Distribution Manager sat in the corner joking with the Product Manager and the Retiring Man about the lines he had been given. "I woke up at about three-thirty in the morning in a cold sweat, repeating my part over and over to myself. I even thought about cue cards."

"Don't worry," the Product Manager said. "We'll cue you at the right time."

Then there was the Assistant Manager. She stood in her appointed place, just where Stanislavski placed her the night before when they blocked the whole thing out. She was looking over various pieces of paper, mumbling her rehearsed lines and preparing for the performance ahead. As Stanislavski approached her, her head cocked up and she smiled.

"Stan," she said, "I'm a bit nervous. I guess I've always suffered from a bit of stage fright."

"No, you'll do just fine. I have worked with thousands of role players like you. I'm confident that you'll do just fine."

Stanislavski spent the last few moments making sure that all of the props were in place including the special lighting they had brought with them. He also spent a few moments concentrating on remaining in character, that of a senior manager in a medium-sized corporation, about to give an important presentation. He was well aware of his motivation.

"They should be here any minute," the Research Manager said to the group. "The CEO's office just called up to let us know that the first group is on the way." Soon, they heard the noise of approaching voices.

"It's about to begin," the Assistant Director said. "Do you have any last words of wisdom, Stan?"

"Break a leg. Places, everyone!"

The Assistant Director, Chief Financial Officer, Distribution Manager, Retired Manager, Customer, Purchasing Manager, and Shopper disappeared from view, and Stanislavski took a place close to where the screen and the computer projection were set up for the initial presentation.

The CEO entered with six other people. What they saw on the dais at the front was a desk on one side and a round conference table on the other side. Each set stood alone and empty except for a halogen lamp placed beside it. The CEO approached Stanislavski and shook his hand in a very businesslike manner. The action was clearly to establish a degree of formality. Stanislavski took the cue and assumed a similarly formal posture as he returned the greeting.

"I see that the stage is set for our production," the CEO said with a defusing smile and a knowing wink to Stanislavski before moving to his place at one of the tables. The rest of the group filled in the other spaces and began to flip through the material which had been placed in front of each chair. Strange looks were exchanged as they studied the books marked *Playbill* which were placed around the tables. The CEO soon raised his voice and asked for everyone's attention.

"Three months ago, I set out to hire a director of marketing who could affect a change here a The Ater Company. I thought I needed to hire someone with a plan. I interviewed a number of candidates. I heard a number of plans. But all I heard were patches not fixes. Then a confident and brazen Stan Islavski stormed into my office and told me he had a method. It wasn't a plan. It was a method, his method, and it was a clearly defined approach to connecting us with customers and markets; audiences as he put it."

The CEO took a sip of water and continued. "Stan helped me understand that in order to address the problems of the company through marketing we need to first tear down our preconceived notions of ourselves and our processes so we could start over from an entirely new perspective; an approach focused on teaching us a renewable method for continually connecting this company with its ever-changing customers and markets."

The CEO took a breath and continued with, "I hired him immediately, and challenged him to develop both a strategic approach to marketing and a marketing plan for this company. Call it a script, one based on Stan's method." He purposely left off the alter-ego last name for fear of giving away the secret too soon. "My goal was," he continued, "for Stan not only to give us direction but to instill in us a foundation for adapting to changing market conditions as we encounter them." The assembled group seemed to be hanging on his every word. He wasn't sure if they were enthralled by his obvious genius or merely confused by his monologue. Undeterred, he pressed on.

"Stan accepted the challenge and today's presentation is the result. What I think you all will hear in today's presentation, is how we can focus at all levels of the company, not only on how we understand the markets we serve, but how we *align* ourselves with those markets and their customers so that we *connect* in a meaningful and renewable way."

The CEO looked in Stan's direction. "So, without further ado, I give you the maestro of marketing, the director himself, Mr. Stan Islavski."

Stanislavski knew how to establish a stage presence. Through years of study he had learned that stage presence is built more by what is *not* done than by what *is* done. He stood in silence for a few moments, just long enough to build a bit of dramatic tension but not long enough to make people think he had forgotten his lines.

"Before being asked to join this company as the Director of Marketing," he began, "My experience was primarily one of helping people to define and perfect roles. My method, one which I have been developing over many years, teaches the unteachable. The method provides its disciples with a technique to employ when playing a role, techniques that lead them to a more complete understanding of the character," he paused reminding himself of his audience before correcting himself, "I mean customer. Under the teachings of my method we learn to align internal resources and capabilities with the expectations of an audience."

Stanislavski, as Stan, paused again for dramatic effect. He couldn't help himself. After a moment he continued. "We have worked through and studied the application of my method over the last three months and used it to draw the many conclusions which the team will discuss with you later. First, however, we will present a review of our process and thinking. Our work, as you will see, is based on the traditional marketing principles of resource planning, research on market needs, trend analyses and the like, but it also introduces some non-traditional approaches to connecting with customers and markets."

As he gestured invitingly with his hands he continued, "Our underlying goal was not to focus on single answer solutions but rather to redefine the way our company approaches marketing. We did this by first working on our company's sense of its *self*, its personality and its positioning." He paused again for effect, "Our goal was both to identify what role we could play in the marketplace and decide how we would play it, and to identify the resources we could bring to bear when connecting with customers. We identified and defined our customers' *actions* along with our own. We read the scenes included in the scripts being written in the marketplace and identified the *beats* along the many *unbroken lines* of both our customers' motivations and of our own. We searched for, and in some cases found, the *supreme objectives* of our playwrights as we acted our way toward the end of each of the scripts we were presented."

At that moment the lights in the room dimmed and the projector went on illuminating Stanislavski who stood between it and the screen. It worked just as he had planned it, as a spotlight.

"Gentlemen and ladies, I believe that it was Shakespeare who said it best. 'The play is the thing' and so, without any further ado, I welcome you to the premiere of The Character of the Customer - a story about acting in a way that brings about a *methodical* change." His emphasis on the word 'methodical' was not lost on the CEO.

As Stanislavski stepped aside into the darkness, a slide appeared on the screen. It read *Act I: Prologue in the Customer's Office*. In the background, the audience of executives could hear the commotion as a group of actors unfamiliar with the subtleties of stage movement made their way onto the stage. "The lines will be a bit wooden," Stanislavski thought to himself, "but I think they'll all play their roles well."

From the darkness to the left of the screen came Stanislavski's voice again, now sounding very much like a narrator standing distant from the main scene of action. "Our story opens as do most marketing stories, with a disconnect between a company and one of its customers."

Scene I: The Customer's Office

(a single light illuminates a desk on the right side of the stage)

(behind the desk sits the Customer, and, sitting in chairs facing the desk, are the Purchasing Manager and the Assistant Director)

Assistant Director (sounding a bit stiff): I'm here because we want to serve you and your customers better. So I have come with this full complement of products and services to sell you. I would appreciate it if you would pick what you want from our product list and I will see to it that our company gets the order out right away.

(she hands one piece of paper to the Customer, and one to the Purchasing Manager)

Customer: This is nice, very comprehensive, but it doesn't help me.

Purchasing Manager: It doesn't help me either.

Assistant Director: Why not? It is a comprehensive list of our products.

Purchasing Manager: Although I am a purchasing manager, there is more to what I do than simply review and purchase your products.

Customer (somewhat overdramatic): We're not connecting. Do you know what its like to be me? To sit here every day and deal with you on one side and my customers on the other?

Assistant Director: So how can I help you?

Customer: I don't know the answer to that. I'm not you. I don't know what you know about you. Let me ask it this way: If you were me, what would you want you to do for you?

(lights fade, new slide moves into position)

Scene II: The Internal Challenge

(lights come up to a conference room table)

(seated at the table are the Communications Manager, Research Manager, Product Manager, and Assistant Director)

Narrator (Stanislavski): What we learned from the prologue was that we shouldn't start with the customer, but rather with ourselves, this company. Experience has taught that, if you don't understand who you are, you'll never know how to play your role. Until you develop an internal understanding of your capabilities and range, you'll keep picking the wrong approach, never succeeding at connecting with your role in the marketplace.

Assistant Director: That's right, he wasn't happy. He actually asked me if I knew what it was like to be him. Like some role playing exercise. He wanted me to be my own customer. I asked him what we could do for him and he asked me the same question right back. It confused me. It occurred to me that I wasn't connected with him. I realized that I had to get into his head and figure out what he wants and why he wants it. I needed to understand his motivation for asking. Truth is I wasn't really sure how to do what I needed to do to connect with him.

Product Manager: But what if you get in there and you find out he wants something we can't do? Or worse, something we can do, but don't know we can do.

(pause)

Assistant Manager: Do we, in the marketing department, really have a sense of who we are as a company and of our range?

Research Manager: There are the results of the last marketing audit...

Assistant Director (interrupting): No, that's not what I'm looking for.

(she stands up and takes center stage)

Assistant Direct (continuing): We need to know more about our *selves* before we can answer this simple question from our customer.

Communications Manager: But who, or what, is the *self* we are talking about here?

Assistant Director: We are talking about the individual *selves* of the company, the individual *selves* that make up the collective *self* of the company. The Chief Financial Officer, for instance, the people in Distribution, they are all a part of the *self*.

(CFO, Distribution Manager and Retiring Man appear from the wings and enter the conversation)

CFO: We are not really sure what the company *self* is either.

Distribution Manager: I thought I knew the range of The Ater Company before I met up with all of you.

Retiring Man: I can tell you a lot about what we have been as a company and what we might be able to become.

Assistant Director: This is clearly a challenge for all of us inside the company. Let's work on it together.

(lights fade to black)

Narrator (Stanislavski): To address the *inner* challenge, our players asked many questions and came to realize that the corporate self of The Ater Company was a collection of the individual contributions that each person, team and department made to the whole. They collected and inventoried the company's capabilities, describing them in terms of how our new marketing method defines actions and motivations. But that wasn't the only challenge they faced.

(slide changes)

Scene III: The External Challenge

(lights come up on the Customer's office)

(sitting at the desk are the Customer and the Assistant Director)

Assistant Director: I think we are part of the way toward answering your question, you know, the one about what we could do for you by putting ourselves in your place. But now we need a bit of your help so that we can help you better.

Customer: What do you need from me?

Assistant Director: We need to understand the character of *you* as a customer and the character of *your* customers.

Customer: If you're talking about market research I've got tons.

Assistant Director: (cutting him off) No, we're looking for things that are based in motivations and objectives.

Customer: Please explain.

Assistant Director: I noticed that there is a shopper over there, returning one of our items. Can we listen in on the conversation?

Customer: That is the kind of problem I'm talking about. You'll see.

(they walk to the other side of the stage, where the Shopper and the Purchasing Manager are speaking to each other)

(the Assistant Director pulls out a notepad and begins taking notes)

Purchasing Manager: I'm sorry to hear that you had this problem and that we were unable to help. I understand that you've tried three other products we carry but that none solved the problem.

Shopper: I've returned all three. I just feel too unsafe having them in the house, with my grandchildren running around as much as they do.

(words appear on screen in handwritten form, as if from the Assistant Director's notes: **to protect my family from harm**)

Purchasing Manager: I'm sorry to hear that. You know we would never sell any product that we felt was unsafe. We work hard to insure that all of the products we carry meet safety standards.

(More words appear on the screen in handwritten form, below the first sentence: **to appease the concern of a customer**)

(Shopper exits)

(Assistant Director and Customer approach)

Customer (to Purchasing Manager): Did you know that customers felt these products were unsafe?

Purchasing Manager: This is the first I have heard of it. I don't think any other employee has heard this complaint.

Customer: Does the concern hold any merit?

Purchasing Manager: Fundamentally, these products are safe. I'm sure that there would have been ways to address her concerns if we had known about them in advance.

(more words appear on the screen in handwritten form, below two earlier sentences: **educating employees about products**)

Customer: Are there other products we might offer instead? What are the alternatives?

Purchasing Manager: There are other products, but we don't carry any of them.

Customer: Why not?

Purchasing Manager: A variety of reasons. Mainly pricing and credit terms. The companies that manufacture them just don't seem to want to make it convenient for us to stock their products.

(a fourth comment appears on the screen in handwritten form: ***making purchasing more convenient***)

Assistant Director: I have been listening to your conversation, and I have observed your *actions*. I think I can help. Take a look at this.

(she shows him the notepad)

Assistant Director: I can help you by answering the concern of a customer about using a product safely. And I can help you by educating your employees about our products and making purchasing more convenient.

(Customer nods as if impressed)

(lights fade)

Narrator (Stanislavski): Now comes the key marketing problem. (pause). How to respond? How do we get to a synthesis, an understanding of who we are as individuals and a company and how we relate to the character and objectives of the customer?

(slide changes and new words appear on the screen)

Scene IV: Synthesis

(lights come up on conference room table)

(around the table are the Communications Manager, Product Manager, Research Manager, CFO and Distribution Manager)

Assistant Director: Okay, we talked to our customers, and our customers' customers, and we now have a sense of the script they are using. We have identified their intentions. We have observed their actions in addition to their behavior.

Research Manager: We've also studied our own actions. We've delved deep into our self. My reports outline intersections of our capabilities and motivations with those of our customers and of our markets.

Retiring Man: So what did you find? I know we all got to meet and got to know some new people, but what is it all about?

CFO: Yeah, how has all of this helped us get closer to a connection with the customer? And when can we talk about pricing?

(CFO winks to the audience who laugh at the momentary break from character)

Assistant Director: I'm glad you've asked.

(she rises from her chair, walks to the projection screen and claps her hands)

(a new slide appears that reads: ***Getting in Line***)

Product Manager: In line after whom?

(group laughs awkwardly)

Assistant Director: Not in line *after*, in line *with*. We now know the intentions of our markets. We know their true actions. We can identify the beats of their roles as they relate to purchase decisions which involve us. Their beats form a line. That line leads from them through the achievement of a supreme objective. Sometimes we are the end of the line and sometimes we're along the line. Our job is to know what the beats are and to help move the consumer forward through their action toward the end of the line.

CFO: What do you mean by that?

Assistant Director: I'll explain, but I'll need some help.

(on cue, the Customer enters with his Purchasing Manager and the Shopper)

Customer: If you are trying to help us, the least we can do is help you in return.

(Assistant Director assembles the cast, one by one, in a single line so the Shopper is at the far

end of the line stage left with the CFO at the far
end stage right)

Research Manager (looking down the line from his
position as third from the end): But where is the Chief
Executive Officer?

(assembled cast looks out into the audience)

This was not a part of the script that the CEO had heard about. Cautiously
he stood, trusting that Stanislavski would not have blocked the scene this
way if it wasn't necessary. He walked to the stage and took his place next
to the CFO. The play resumed.

(Assistant Director leaves the line and walks to
the Shopper)

Assistant Director: What is the action in your purchase which is
not being completed?

Shopper: To protect my family from harm.

Assistant Director (to the others): Who can help?

Communications Manager (stepping forward): Now that I
understand your motivation, I can. You see, our product meets all
safety standards. But we don't communicate it effectively enough.
I will meet you at that beat and move you to the next point on the
way to your objective, which is to purchase a safe product.

(the two leave the stage, continuing their
conversation)

(Assistant Director walks to the Purchasing Manager)

Assistant Director: Please state your action.

Purchasing Manager: To make purchasing more convenient.

Assistant Director: Who can help?

Distribution Manager (stepping forward): Now that I understand your motivation, I can modify our delivery procedures to meet you at that beat. But I can't do it under our current cost and price structure. Can anyone help me?

CFO (stepping forward): Now that I understand your motivation, I can adapt our cost allocation system to allow you to amortize your distribution costs differently and maintain your unit costs, if that helps. But to do it I will need certain concessions from our suppliers. Can anyone help me?

Retiring Man (stepping forward): Now that I understand your motivation, I will meet you at that beat by negotiating contracts that will provide the concessions you need to accommodate distribution to satisfy the objective of the customer.

(the three convene in the middle of the stage, shake hands and then exit together)

(Assistant Director walks to the Customer)

Assistant Director: What is your action?

Customer: To educate my sales people about products and dispel the concerns of my customers.

Product Manager (stepping forward) : Now that I understand your motivation, I can help. I can provide detailed information about our products and I can construct programs to make it readily accessible to your employees. But I don't know about the details of other products.

Research Manager: I do. Now that I understand your motivation, I can tell you more than you ever wanted to know about the other products. In fact, through my research, I can also tell you the profiles of the customers.

Product Manager: And, with that information, I can modify our product bundles to address those concerns.

In Unison: Now that we understand each other's motivations, let's beat it.

(the three convene in the middle of the stage, shake hands and exit together to the left)

(Narrator enters the stage, standing between the CEO and the Assistant Director, who remain front and center)

Narrator (to Assistant Director): You've been the representative of Corporate Marketing during this production. What is your action?"

Assistant Director (after pause): My action is to play my role in the company by connecting our internal resources with the external motivations of our customers so we achieve synthesis with the marketplace and are aligned with the *character of our customers.*

Narrator: Can anyone help with this objective?

(pause as characters wait for the CEO to speak)

The remaining cast turned and stared at the CEO. It was clear to everyone that Stanislavski expected the CEO to improvise. Thinking quickly was one of his strengths and Stanislavski knew it. In fact he had counted on it. The CEO immediately responded as if he had had the script in advance.

CEO: I can. Now that I understand your motivation, I can meet you at that beat and move us down the line," he answered. "I can create an environment where we encourage interaction and support experimentation with ideas and approaches. I can see to it that this is a company where the players are encouraged to rehearse, where they are blocked when necessary and allowed to improvise when appropriate. I can also be sure that the emotion memory of this place is preserved and passed down. I can be sure that we continue this performance into the future.

Assistant Director: I'm beat. Let's get out of here.

(Assistant Director takes CEO's hand in one of her hands and Narrator's in the other and walks them off stage smiling)

(slide changes to read: ***The Beginning ...***)

The audience of executives, advisors and directors laughed at the suggestion of the last slide and applauded enthusiastically.

At the end of the performance, the lights came up, and the Assistant Director stepped forward as the others took their seats. "What you have just experienced is the foundation of our new method for connecting with the character of our customers here in marketing. We have found that there are many scripts in the market and in each one our customers play a different role, and they display different actions, even if the behavior is the same. The real question for us is: *How do we continually adapt and connect with the main characters in the constantly changing scripts in the marketplace?* And that leads us to ask: *What technique can we use to insure continued alignment and synthesis?*"

With that the Assistant Director began her portion of the formal presentation. Her voice was stronger than it had been at the rehearsal, but Stanislavski knew she was overcompensating for a bit of nervousness. When the questions started coming, her comfort level improved dramatically. "Part of her character," Stanislavski said to himself. "She's a fighter." Like a good musician in an improviser role, she continued to roll out the insights into a structure that gave them better life and stronger meaning. Throughout her presentation she referred to the method using terms like alignment, range and supreme objective. Without even realizing it, she had become an actor in the CEO's production and she was playing her part brilliantly.

Stanislavski exhaled deeply, finally feeling a bit relaxed. He had taught them his method and they had learned it well. The method had worked. With just a bit of adaptation it had applied itself to the marketing

177

process. The method had answered many questions for this company and the questions it didn't answer were at least demarcated in a fashion that allowed answers to be filled into the blank spaces. With his method in hand, the marketing department of The Ater Company was equipped to connect with the character of their customers. The direction was set, now it was time to let his actors act and let the production unfold for the captive audience. Before he knew it, the lights in the conference room when up to full. The CEO was smiling broadly.

"That was some great work Stan. Bravo."

"Thank you, sir."

As Stanislavski continued shaking hands with the other members of the *audience*, the doors to the meeting room flung open, revealing the Deli Owner. He and a few of the people from his deli rolled in all sorts of food and coffee for the crowd, including sour cream and onion potato chips. The Deli Owner's voice registered on Stanislavski's ears the moment he walked through the door.

"Stan! The Man from Moscow! How are you doing?"

He approached the place where Stanislavski and the CEO stood. He stretched out his other hand, asking "How did it go?"

Stanislavski gestured over to the CEO and waited for his review. "Marvelous," the CEO commented, leaning over to Stanislavski. He continued, secretively. "I think I can finally erase the whiteboard."

"You see," the Deli Owner said, gently poking Stanislavski in the ribs. "I taught you everything you needed to know about marketing."

Stanislavski leaned forward, quietly asking the Deli Owner, "Did you bring the..."

Before he could finish the question, the Deli Owner reached under one of his rolling tray cabinets to reveal a bouquet of roses.

"Who are the flowers for?" asked the CEO.

Stanislavski took them from the Deli Owner. "For the leading lady, of course," he said as he turned and handed them to the Assistant Director.

She blushed as the Deli Owner reached over the table to shake her hand in congratulations. The flowers allowed Stanislavski to turn the attention from him to her, and he slipped into the background while she answered final questions about the performance.

After lunch, the CEO clapped his hands to make an announcement. "I'd like to suggest we take a break and come back to address the implications of this presentation, but I'm going to ask the marketing team, or, troupe, shall I say," he smiled at Stanislavski, "to leave us for this part of the discussion. We'll ask you back in about 30 minutes to ask some more questions."

"You're just trying to steal all of the pastries and coffee for yourselves," the Product Manager complained lightheartedly.

"I'll save some for you, don't worry," the Deli Owner responded. "You could afford to loose a few pounds, anyway."

As another round of coffee was distributed to the assembled crowd of senior management and advisors, the marketing troupe left the room. Outside, the Assistant Director caught up with Stanislavski and pulled him aside to ask how he thought it went. Instead of hearing a review of her performance from the master Director, she was in for some surprising news.

"How do you think it went," she asked a bit nervously.

"Very well," he said, "better than I would have imagined." He paused and took a breath, and decided it was time to tell her the truth about who he was so that she would be prepared for the decision that was to come.

"There is something I have not been permitted to tell you, but, now that I am the end of my three month assignment, I can explain it. You see, I'm not really a marketing professional. I am a director and actor. I accidentally came in for an interview because I thought they were interviewing for a theater director, not a marketing director. But your CEO and I hit it off almost immediately. We decided to try this experiment and see how it worked."

"Part of the experiment, though," he continued, "had to do with your professional progress. He felt that you were the right person for my position, but you hadn't had the experience or vision yet to bring it all together. Clearly, the presentation you just gave demonstrates that ability. Not only are they deciding on our marketing plan, but they are also deciding on the position of marketing director, and I think you are going to get it." He gently put his hand on her shoulder in a very paternal sort of way, ready now to tell her the complete truth.

"My real name is Constantin Stanislavski, not Stan Islavski." The blank stare in her eyes betrayed her new found confidence.

"I am the founder and father of Method Acting. I developed the *method* over many years as a way to help teach an intangible. My method is a system actors use to connect with the characters they were portraying and bring life to productions in a way that aligns their individual *selves* with the *beats* of the script in an effort to *align* the cast such that they would deliver an inspiring production to an audience anxious to consume the material and see how it ends.

He waited anxiously for the reaction that was sure to come from his new friend and protégé.

The Assistant Director looked at Stan with an expressionless gaze that worried Stan a bit. After a few seconds the corners of her mouth curled up into a big, inviting smile.

"Now it all makes sense," she said dramatically as she gave him a big hug and a gentle kiss on the check.

Epilogue

Six Months Later

Stanislavski knocked on the door of his old office at The Ater Company. He looked at the new brass nameplate on the door, listing the name of his former Assistant Director except with a new title: Director of Marketing. He noticed that the director part of the title came first, as he felt it should.

"Constantin, it's great to see you!"

She came over to the door with a smile on her face. "I see you've gotten used to calling me by my real name," he commented. "I guess I'm a bit sorry to see that character fade into my list of former roles."

"The way I hear it, Stan's not dead yet. I understand your consulting practice is doing very well."

"Actually, it is. I've expanded my business beyond just marketing. It seems that the method has broad application in many areas of business and corporate operations. It all started when I signed up your Customer as my first client about a month after the presentation. I knew there was a good reason to include him in the play we did. I also wanted you to be the first to know, I've decided to write a series of books chronicling my experiences as a 'method consultant'.

"That's great, *Stan*," she said drawing out the Stan as a humorous dig at his alter ego. "I'll write the forward."

"I'd like that," he said. "But for now, let's just go get some lunch."

She put on her coat and they headed to the elevator.

"I have more exciting news," he said nonchalantly as they walked. He paused for just the right amount of time to build anticipation for his big announcement. "I've just been given the opportunity to become a founding partner in a community theater operation. Our first production is going to be Othello. Looks like I'll finally get to apply some of what I've learned here to the theater!"

"I can't wait to see how it ends," responded the Assistant Director as she locked arms with him and together they stepped onto the elevator.